THINKING
ABOUT
COHOUSING

the creation of
intentional neighbourhoods

Martin Field

Diggers & Dreamers Publications First Published 2004
www.diggersanddreamers.org.uk
ISBN 0-9514945-7-0 Paperback
Distribution : Edge of Time Ltd
BCM Edge London WC1N 3XX www.edgeoftime.co.uk
Printing :Lightening Source : www.lighteningsource.co.uk
Design & Layout : Catandcoat :www.catandcoat.co.uk

Acknowledgements

This book has been a long time in the making. My thanks and gratitude need to be registered for the patience the Diggers & Dreamers Editors have had with me (especially Chris), while the chapters labouriously took their very hesitant shapes; and to Jay for her faith in me when the task sometimes seemed to commandeer our life.

My thanks to Maria, Lucy, Sarah, Chris and Steve for their contributions I hope the final work makes up for the delay!

Also to Andy, Lucy N, Chris C and Chris M and Mary for the formative debates we had during the short life of the Foundation.

A fair part of the material had a beginning in work undertaken in the School of Architecture and Building Engineering at the University of Liverpool, and I also thank colleagues there for their interest and support over the years.

Finally my thanks to the many CoHousing and community groups who have all helped to shape the content of the following pages through them sharing their insights and experiences with me.

All Photos - by the author

It might be thought that UK Government policy on sustainable communities should offer a clear support for the aspirations of community-minded groups seeking to create new neighbourhoods in which they could live. That there still remains such little experience of new neighbourhood development being led by the households that will reside in them suggests this is still far from being common.

This book examines the potential of CoHousing in the UK, and how it stands out from other models of neighbourhood development(s) in offering a very tangible route towards the creation of new and 'sustainable' neighbourhoods. It seeks to provide practical and strategic advice to those whose ambition is to turn the concept of CoHousing into a new neighbourhood reality, and to those who could give their support to such ambition.
It will examine:

- the 'identity' of the UK CoHousing 'world'
- what assists or impedes making new communities
- the development of mixed tenure communities
- how CoHousing & communal living arrangement could fit within wider UK housing and design developments

The material includes consideration of what motivates the formal agencies that routinely involve themselves in new community projects, plus some examination of where and how public resources are usually directed. Lastly the book encourages CoHousing Groups to evaluate their own resources and at times, limitations, through a series of practical frameworks developed to cultivate a methodical approach to satisfying each necessary step of the development process.

The development of modern 'sustainable' communities and the planning of ambitious new settlements (like Poundbury) is clearly set to continue. This publication should complement such high-level initiatives by its focus on communities at street-level. CoHousing provides a very real blueprint around which new neighbourhoods will thrive, once opportunities have been provided for their creation.

CONTENTS

Over the past 150 years, the UK has been host to an evolving and colourful creation of new communities and innovative neighbourhood environments. Local housing developments were pioneered by house-building co-operatives, set up to fund and build properties for their members and families. Socialist and utopian groups set up new communities to have explicitly egalitarian and non-exploitative lifestyles. There was the philanthropic town-planning of visionary industrialists such as Rowntree and Cadbury, who sought to foster a vibrant community ethos within innovative & self-supporting suburban developments. Finally there was the Garden Cities movement, inspired by Ebenezer Howard, which extended this community development focus across a wide range of urban and suburban settings, and which sought to provide a radical new model for planning new urban areas. Its legacy remains influential, both in the community detail explored by Coates (2001), and in its intellectual vigour that Ward & Hall (1998) have used to challenge modern assumptions about city growth. The success of such development, at least in terms of popularising housebuilding for new settlements, led in no small part to the massive development of state-funded 'council housing' throughout the UK, and ultimately nurtured the New Towns programme in which to settle, and at times resettle, the nation's sprawling population.

These early initiatives had been more than just an approach to solving housing needs. Explicit in the 'utopian' and socialist aspirations of the 19th and early 20thCenturies communities described by Pearson (1995) and Hardy (2001), was the desire to share local facilities in such neighbourhoods, beyond merely living on the same street or in the same building. This desire has been echoed by the substantial number of co-operatives, communes and other egalitarian groups (like squatter initiatives) started in the 1960s & 70s (see Neville 1974). Some were clearly attempts to turn to 'shared living' in the context of a wider but less flexible contemporary society, although a number were developed as specific reactions against the intervention of central government plans. The extent and effect that government plans to demolish older housing stock accommodated the changing fashions for town planning & estate improvements have been the subject of many commentators from Turner (1972), Seabrook (1984), Ward (1985), to Young & Lemos (1997). It is salutatory that so many have commented on the consequence that such redevelopment had on local communities, especially to diminish previous neighbourhood identities.

It is more than interesting, therefore, that the concept of 'community' appears to have such a central role in a great deal of current discussion about the merits or challenges of the contemporary social environment. In key government policy initiatives - Urban and Rural White Papers, consultation papers for Planning and Health service reforms, and high-profile regeneration imperatives like 'Urban Renaissance', 'neighbourhood renewal' and 'social exclusion' - the concept of 'community' is put forward as a central value around which so much effort should revolve. A publication like the DETR's (2000) Millennium Villages and Sustainable Communities is explicit in putting a positive worth on connecting a sense of modern 'community' with the policy imperative to promote 'sustainability' in new settlements. It is not necessarily clear, however, what are the key features or characteristics of such 'community', nor whether a particular action or combination of actions will result in a 'community' being created, or strengthened, or made 'sustainable'. Much is usually written about key elements to 'sustain' the life of a community - usually in terms of the economic factors like income and work, or the potential for addressing environmental issues, like energy supply and waste management and local transport, or the deciding factors of the local housing market. Much less is heard about what nurtures the life of actual households within the neighbourhood area identified as the community environment they could regard as 'home'.

Often the concept (and particularly the perceived lack) of what is essential to a healthy 'community' seems to come forward within wider debates on 'social exclusion', invoked to describe something pathological or damaged within parts of our towns or cities. Attention is perennially focused upon addressing what has appeared to have broken down within the social relationships of such areas. It is, however, not clear what models of relationships are being used as the yardstick against which such examination is done. Contemporary writers on housing policies like Balchin (1995) & Brown (1999) explore the role for housing resources to administer to ailing or needy households, but offer little comment of what basic housing approaches could do to support alternative community-minded ideals. Consideration on the provision of new neighbourhoods seems at best a rehearsal of views for where this might be arranged. The debate between Schoon & Hall (2002) about accommodating urban growth in 'new towns' or through the masterplanning of 'urban extensions' is a debate about spatial preferences, rather than a re-evaluation of the process for how new neighbourhoods are built. Too often the sole inclusion of local people in such processes is via some general 'consultation' exercise focused upon broad principles of land allocation rather than upon eliciting clear statements of local residents' desires.

What is absent from much discussion of 'community' initiatives is a sufficient understanding of what impact can be achieved through the presence of 'intentionality' in neighbourhood communities - i.e. what has brought a household or group of households to that location in the first place. At least one major recent attitudinal survey has pointed to how 'belonging to a community' seems integral to individual personal well-being (see www.wellbeing.com/survey2002) yet an awareness of this interest in deliberately 'collective' living arrangements is largely absent from the wider debate on 'community' well-being. A shared desire for some kind of 'intentional community ' - a collective or collaborative approach to neighbourhood life alongside similarly-minded others - has clearly underpinned the development of the 'utopian' models of the communities like the inter-war example of the Isokon project in Highgate (see also Hardy, Coates et al). It is not, however, something confined to the past. The continual setting-up of new communities and new communal groups over the past few years, as documented by periodicals like Diggers & Dreamers, is ample demonstration of the interest in innovative or collective living arrangements. (And while it has recorded the vast majority, the Directory still makes no attempt to call itself a completely comprehensive record of all the communal living groups in the UK!). A particular inspiration to many of the new groups is that of CoHousing - a contemporary model for modern intentional neighbourhoods. The successful ability of such neighbourhoods to mix private and communal life confidently together have become powerful attractions to people searching for modern flexible living arrangements.

CoHousing brings a deceptive simplicity to the business of creating new communities - either in new or existing neighbourhoods. It is rooted in the successful developments of 'intentional communities' abroad, where a strong body of CoHousing practice has established clearly successful neighbourhoods that are still thriving years after being established. For example, the Danish CoHousing community at Jystrup still had two-thirds of its original member-households twenty years after its conception and creation, and a waiting list from second-generation households : it would be interesting to see what contemporary housing settings could demonstrate that degree of stability. CoHousing is able to do this partly because it is clear about how to support an intention to create a shared neighbourhood and partly because it is a recognisable alternative to the orthodoxy of so much modern housing that only caters for separate nuclear households.

To hear CoHousing described, however, is not always to hear what stands it apart from other settings for collective living. It has been variously likened to a modern form of co-operative accommodation, or shared accommodation, or as an ecovillage, or as a new idea for a commune - or some other combination(s) of such terms. None of this helps those new to the concept to be clear about just what CoHousing offers to communities, nor how to know where this is distinguishable from other community ideas. There are also core elements of a CoHousing neighbourhood without all of which, it will not function as a CoHousing enterprise and, in all likelihood, the neighbourhood will not demonstrate the kind of qualities that has attracted people to the concept in the first place.

A straightforward description of CoHousing would be that it is a particular style of neighbourhood development, based upon a creative combination of private and communal facilities. It is less than straightforward, however, to believe that the use of the term CoHousing is synonymous with a clear understanding of what CoHousing is supposed to represent. A colleague reported to me a meeting with members of a new CoHousing group from the Midlands area. Their conversation noted that the plans of some UK CoHousing groups did not seem to include much immediate intention to share meals together. *"That's because eating together isn't a big part of CoHousing"*, said one of the Midlands group. Needless to say, the remark was firmly challenged by others who put their colleague straight on this having played a fundamental part in the evolution of many CoHousing communities. Such a comment does invite contemplation, however, on the general level of awareness of how CoHousing is really understood in the UK. The use of the term CoHousing too often seems to be a catch-all description for 'how people-might-share-some-communal-life-together'. Barton(2000) simply describes CoHousing as a 'way of building a close-knit ecological community', which he then goes on to discuss in terms of localised energy and waste treatment systems! If a proper understanding of CoHousing developments is to recognise essential distinctions from other ideas of sustainable neighbourhoods, it will be important to clarify what is essential for a community to actually be a CoHousing one.

An appreciation of this first point - the essentials of a

CoHousing community - is not difficult to achieve. A number of clear descriptions of CoHousing principles and developments already exist, along with a mass of detail that document and display successful CoHousing neighbourhoods [see Bibliography]. What may be less easy is to contrast the core elements of CoHousing with other aspirations for neighbourhood developments in the UK. The approach taken here is therefore to:

>a) provide a summary of what CoHousing is, by way of defining its key principles,
>
>b) list other housing, neighbourhood and communal living schemes that differ from CoHousing by one or other of the above principles;
>
>c) summarise the distinctive differences of CoHousing neighbourhoods from other community orientated settings.

What CoHousing is

The work of McCamant & Durrett (1988, 1994), Fromm (1991), Zahle and Mortensen (1992) and Hanson (1996) has all been fundamental in clarifying the core principles that underpin CoHousing communities :

>(a) Designing for intentional neighbourhoods
>
>(b) The minimum provision of private and common facilities
>
>(c) Size and scale to support communitydynamics
>
>(d) Residents' control and management

(a) Designing for intentional neighbourhoods

In the main, CoHousing communities have been developed within their own discrete neighbourhoods, which have a physical layout that makes deliberate use of architectural and design features to maximise intentional and incidental social contact between the people living there. An example will be in deliberately siting some of those internal rooms in private homes where people spend a significant amount of indoors-time (like kitchen areas) to be outward-looking towards communal spaces outside where their neighbours might be walking or relaxing. This will generate spontaneous opportunities for residents to have visual or verbal contact together, and exploit natural opportunities to communicate and socialise together.

The overall setting of CoHousing neighbourhoods are invariably completely vehicle-free, with the use of any cars kept to parking or garage areas at the edge of the site, which is given over to a thoroughly pedestrianised character. There may or may not be some small garden areas for the private use of each household, however these will only be modest in size in order to encourage neighbours to meet and mix together in the neighbourhood's shared open and recreational spaces.

(b) The minimum provision of private and common facilities

All households in CoHousing neighbourhoods have private and self-contained accommodation - i.e. they all have private and sole use of their own domestic living, eating, cooking and washing spaces. This is, however, supplemented by other facilities within the CoHousing neighbourhood that can be shared and used by all the CoHousing households - for example laundry facilities, guest accommodation, or rooms for craft and hobby activities. (Some CoHousing settings even have barns, greenhouses, garages, workshops, and ground for sports!)

The design and location of a common building is a key venue for such communal facilities and other leisure activities open to all the community. While there is no standard blueprint for such common facilities, a minimum would be facilities to allow for the preparation and enjoyment of sharing meals and be of a sufficient size for all the households and community members to meet together for joint activities, whenever this is desired.

(c) Size and scale to support community dynamics

CoHousing communities have recognised that there is an important careful balance to achieve between creating a common identity in a neighbourhood's residents alongside sustaining a sufficient level of privacy for each household in that neighbourhood. There is no intention to live in one another's pockets the whole time! In practice, this means that the sizes of CoHousing communities recognise that the scale of each community has to pay attention to its personal dimensions - to how big or how small it is. There is a recognition that the number of households needs to accommodate times when some may choose to be private and not feel obliged to participate in communal activities, without their absence constraining other communal activities or contact. There is, however, also the recognition that the total size of the neighbourhood population should enable all members to know one another personally through communal activities and other incidental contact, and not be so large a group that such familiarity is too difficult to sustain.

A rule-of-thumb from Danish commentators is that, in practice, the number of adults in a community should range between about ten and forty. Individual households will obviously vary in their complete make-up of ages and sizes.

(d) Residents' control and management

The residents of a CoHousing neighbourhood are always responsible for all the aspects of its creation and operation. This will start in managing the formalities of the planning, design and finances that will be inevitably required at each stage of the community's development, and could include making professional appointments to carry out the different construction, legal and technical necessities of such development.

The residents are then collectively responsible for managing the neighbourhood and its facilities. There is no distinction, for example by the individual tenure each household may have on their property (i.e. ownership, rental, etc.). All the households jointly decide how to choose new member-households from those wishing to join the neighbourhood in the future, if and when such an opportunity arises. All households are likely to share the basic costs of the basic communal facilities, notwithstanding how they may choose whether or not to join in a particular communal activity on a given day.

What CoHousing is not

By the essential nature of its basic characteristics CoHousing neighbourhoods demonstrate a singular approach to creating a supportive environment for how and where households can relate to one another on a day-by-day basis. Without all of these required features, however, CoHousing could not hope to transcend the limits inherent in many other neighbourhood settings:

> (a) the limits to, and limitations of, space and privacy, common to housing co-operatives or communes;
> (b) the limits inherent in the planning of social or pri vate housing estates, designed principally as com modities to satisfy immediate markets, rather than to foster long-term community well-being;
> (c) the limits to 'sustainable' initiatives, that do not understand how to match a community's interper sonal dynamics alongside concerns about the natural environment.

All the core characteristics of CoHousing neighbourhoods noted above need to be present to establish a community setting as a CoHousing development. The omission of any one will lead to a separate dynamic of communal development different from a recognisably CoHousing dynamic. That this is an essential feature of what makes the setting a CoHousing one, does not always register within the descriptions offered by a variety of commentators. CoHousing has been described to this author as many different things, sometimes, it has seemed, in such a way as to minimise the implied distinctiveness of CoHousing from some other initiative. Yet often neither the description nor the comparable initiative has properly represented a CoHousing community at all.

Often such other 'initiatives' are focused upon 'community-based' developments, yet are too big or too small to function as the basis for a CoHousing neighbourhood. Sometimes the neighbourhood does not have the combination of self-contained accommodation and communal facilities noted above. At other times there is not private self-contained accommodation provided for every household. And very often the decision-making authority over a neighbourhood does not reside with the neighbourhood's households but through the ultimate veto of some external body like a Housing Association.

Listed below is a summary, in no particular order of merit, of housing or communal living arrangements that should be acknowledged, for one reason or the other, as being distinct from CoHousing communities.

(a) Communes and communal living

The necessary combination of fully self-contained accommodation and other common facilities generally sets CoHousing apart from most of the collective living groups who have regularly featured as contemporary communes in the Diggers & Dreamers Directory. Self-contained space, as in each household having private and sole use of living, eating, cooking and washing room, is found in all CoHousing settings, yet is a rare feature in UK communes.

Places like Holtsfield in South Wales, like other old 'plotlands' developments, may be very Arcadian, but are not comprised of fully self-contained accommodation, nor do they have sufficient internal common space in which all the community can gather, nor are they in ultimate control of their own destiny. Even those with extensive facilities for collective use - (refurbished manors with outbuildings and large grounds, like at Old Hall in Suffolk or Lauriston Hall in Scotland) have not been able to provide self-contained accommodation for all their member-households. Various communal settings that might be have been thought of as bone fide CoHousing communities will not pass this test of providing the required private and shared spaces.

Being able to cultivate sufficient personal space within a collective environment shared between a like-minded group is acknowledged as a modern Holy Grail sought by many existing communes. Examples of communal living that have provided this mix are Canon Frome in Somerset and Thundercliffe Grange in South Yorkshire.

(b) Group living schemes & other intentional groups

The scale and collective self-management of CoHousing neighbourhoods sets clear parameters against which other kinds of 'group living' arrangements can be compared. For example a small scheme for four households developed a few years ago in Sheffield, or a shared arrangement for two households in Norway, when matched both against the scale of original Danish communities and against contemporary North American communities, would not be considered sufficient to sustain CoHousing dynamics. A balance between private and shared activity, able to take place at a spontaneous but comfortable pace, involves all residents at some times but without them feeling always obliged to do so. This is simply not possible to sustain in a comfortable way when there are small numbers, where the absence of one household can be so immediately noticeable.

Some communal settings have characteristics that are very close to CoHousing characteristics, albeit without having prioritised such characteristics in any deliberate way. The Alternative Technology Centre at Machnylleth is one example, having self-contained accommodation for its main resident staff plus a number of other shared facilities. The Findhorn Community in Scotland is another, being a mix between commune and self-contained living - although interestingly a group has been looking for some time at the possibility of setting up a CoHousing community outside the Findhorn community's main site.

Other shared communities do exist, like Steiner schools or other residential community-settings for disabled people. Usually, however, not only do these involve people sharing living accommodation, they also have a background ideology different to the collective and egalitarian responsibility of CoHousing, for how, when and why people come to live together.

(c) Village life

To some people, descriptions of CoHousing communities sound like a modern version of life in a small village. While it is not impossible that the local social environment of a CoHousing neighbourhood might develop something of that geographical character, especially if it has been built slightly removed from other properties, there is a clear difference between CoHousing settings and actual villages, and it relates to 'intentionality'. For all the potential Arcadian loveliness of small villages or rural CoHousing development, people are coming to CoHousing schemes specifically to share in a kind of community life, and shared identity. They are wishing to do things together with other people, and to take a shared responsibility for it all. As much as that could be a factor in some people wishing to live in an established village, it would be wrong to think that is what brings everybody to live in one. The appeal of 'village life' does seem for some people that they could 'get away from' others. Such a motivation for being amongst 'village life' (however realistic or unrealistic this may be) will be quite the opposite from deliberately wishing to see more of one's CoHousing neighbours!

Older village -type developments that were challenges to the orthodoxy of their day, like the suburban developments of the Garden Cities, or anarchist land settlements like Whiteways in Gloucestershire, have steadily moved away from the focus on a shared community ethos that is so central to modern CoHousing principles. (They are also of a size that questions their ability to sustain the relationships that CoHousing can support, usually being substantially larger than the indicative range of adults noted above).

(d) New settlements, Urban Villages, etc.

A variety of plans exist around in the UK for whole new urban/suburban settlements, urban villages or urban extensions. The Rowntree Foundation, for example, is developing plans for their New Earswick scheme, as a modern counterpart to their philanthropic developments of the 19th and 20th centuries. To date such plans are not of a quality that could be described as CoHousing development, and it will be interesting to see to what extent the final planning is able to move away from the legacy of UK housing designs that routinely accentuate the privacy of residents from their neighbours.

Some new kinds of urban neighbourhood areas are being built to demonstrate that they can do more than simply provide boxes for people to live in. For example the 'Homes for Change' development in Manchester has combined integral workspaces with the provision of new homes, and has therefore developed a strong urban identity for its member-households. The designs of 'Homes for the Future' in Glasgow have also looked to set a variety of ultra-modern housing designs within a more people-focused local environment. There has not, however, been the provision for other social facilities or interactions, nor the collective control and management over the developed areas that would qualify them as CoHousing neighbourhoods.

It is interesting to note that at least one new urban development - for properties on wasteland by the waterfront in Gateshead - appears to be drawing on design ideas that have much in common with principles of CoHousing design. The designers are being deliberate in hoping to maximise the opportunities for intentional contact between the resident households, not least through providing an overall pedestrianised environment. What is not disputable, however, is that this has come through the involvement of a high profile designer seeking to explore ideas for community-centred architecture, rather than an outcome from the articulated demands of people wishing to live in that new area development.

(e) Ecological developments

Mention has already been made above of describing CoHousing as an 'ecological' approach to community development. There is certainly a potentially strong overlap between CoHousing principles and other ecological or environmental proposals (for example for the relative ease in which an 'ecovillage' could be designed upon CoHousing lines). In as much as both could be based upon desires for the built environment to be environmentally sustainable, and local or self-sustaining systems of energy, water and waste treatments are set up to service the set number of households - all could certainly combine CoHousing principles with the environmental management ones. (with the one proviso that if an ecovillage plan was for large numbers of households within one settlement then this could be developed through a number of mini-neighbourhoods each set up as CoHousing 'parts' within the wider whole.) The low impact development at Tinkers Bubble, as promoted by Fairlie (1996), could eventually combine with all the features essential to a CoHousing neighbourhood. It is a goal of some CoHousing groups to develop in ways that will minimise the impact upon the local natural environment. There is nothing essential, however, about CoHousing having to embrace such ecological principles for energy or waste use, nor for the 'ecological' principles to embrace CoHousing as the means to set up the social environment for wider sustainable human relationships. The pragmatics of subsequent development is likely to dictate the degree of support that CoHousing Groups are able to give to other 'ecological' principles. It may be too difficult to combine a rigorous 'eco-approach' to some urban sites if there is in reality a limited budget to renovate existing buildings in a sensitive ecologically-based manner.

The links between the two sets of ideals may make sense, and may well appeal in the future to households currently only familiar with one set of values. The compatibility of the ideas is nevertheless not a sufficient reason to confuse the descriptions or the terminologies - calling CoHousing communities 'ecological communities' is unnecessary and obfuscates what is distinctive to each.

Other explicit modern 'ecological' developments in the UK, such as the sustainable housing project at Hockerton, or the BedZed minimal-energy development in Croydon, are all fascinating pointers to the future variety of different ecological approaches to small-scale development. They do not, however, come into the category of CoHousing development. There is not the provision of facilities for social and neighbourhood contact that would be intended for CoHousing interaction - rather the properties are focused principally upon the needs of the private households, albeit with massive provision for a sharing of energy and waste use.

(f) Housing Co-operatives

Existing housing co-operatives are extremely unlikely to qualify as CoHousing bodies. It is something of an irony that modern co-operatives could aspire to operate in the spirit of CoHousing principles, yet are likely to be severely in their material opportunities to achieve such an outcome in practice. Modern co-operatives are either: groups of separate households with a well-defined collective identity where each has a self-contained dwelling, but not the communal space or shared facilities necessary to a CoHousing identity, as noted above; or a communal group sharing a single property, without self-contained accommodation for everyone, but with a mixture of other shared facilities.

Some 'co-ops' are registered as housing co-operatives in a very formal sense as Industrial & Provident Societies, which carefully define their egalitarian qualities and frameworks. Other co-ops are merely jointly operated groups that see themselves as seeking a generally co-operative way of life.

In short the characteristics of being a co-operative cross all sorts of distinctions about legal set-ups, buildings, facilities, egalitarianism and shared ambitions. It is now possible for a CoHousing Group to be formally registered as a Housing Co-operative while they develop a recognisably CoHousing neighbourhood. A co-operative group could develop a recognisable CoHousing neighbourhood in the fullness of time, if it develops the required mixture of facilities.

(g) Housing Associations

The definition and role of a Housing Association is basically that of being a body regulated to provide housing accommodation to those in need, operating under clear and explicit guidelines and procedures laid down by the appropriate national regulatory body, currently the Housing Corporation. Importantly, an Association is a body managed and operated to provide accommodation to, and on behalf of, others. The main decision-making bodies of such organisations - the formal Board of Directors - cannot benefit from the operations of their organisation (this generally applies to an Association's paid officers as well). Which particularly means that they cannot secure accommodation from their own body. A CoHousing body, set up to be run by and for its own members, is therefore not going to use the formalities of becoming a Housing Association, because there are fundamental restrictions to how it could support the intended lifestyle of its community members.

[A Housing Association could support the development of a CoHousing scheme, particularly if there is an intention to secure public funds for some of the dwellings. There are, however, a whole series of issues to explore for how the intentions of such formal bodies could co-exist in a joint development with such a self-managed approach as that of a CoHousing Group. See the work of the OWCH group.]

While Housing Associations in general can point to an active involvement in all kinds of 'community oriented' initiatives, for a variety of reasons this will not amount to functioning CoHousing communities. For example, the 'mutual aid' initiative set up by Manningtree Housing Association in Bradford could appear to have a similar ethos of involvement and sharing between local residents. It is, however, only one element in sustaining natural communications between local neighbours, and has not been set in the context of a complete self-managed neighbourhood. Similarly the interest in the Housing Association world for tenants to be involved in the allocation of empty properties - based on developments from Delft in Holland - is not sufficient to be classed as CoHousing, although this was the interpretation made by one Editor of a national Housing periodical.

(h) Home Zones

The contemporary UK promotion of Home Zones, as local initiatives to limit the speed, use, or presence of vehicles in small neighbourhood areas, clearly has some affinity with those CoHousing communities who have relegated vehicular activity to parking areas well away from the domestic dwellings. Certainly this philosophy could be conducive to the creation or existence of other associated local initiatives designed in part to strengthen local identity - like Neighbourhood Watch. The Home Zone approach by itself, however, is not predicated upon local households having to 'sign up' to other values designed to create an explicit collective or intentional neighbourhood environment.

(i) Gated communities

Perhaps because CoHousing has lately been embraced in a big way by community groups in the North America, there is some confusion that the local management by CoHousing households of their neighbourhood is a move towards 'gated communities' that limit or prevent non-residents from entering an exclusive residential area. CoHousing communities would certainly feel that the awareness and contact between its member households means it is relatively easy to be aware of someone being in the neighbourhood who is not from one of the families there. This can be of particular help in being aware of the potential for intruders who may be up to mischief. It should not, however, be a reason to dismiss CoHousing as an excuse for community exclusivity - many communities deliberately want to connect with the wider social environment around the CoHousing homes, in order to see their families ultimately thrive in the opportunities offered by, and given to, that wider milieu.

(j) A selective solution for some needs

CoHousing is already being considered in some quarters as offering the potential answer to a range of emerging community needs. One School of Architecture in London, in reviewing the projected increase in single-person households in the coming years, has proposed a role for CoHousing to help meet the social and housing needs of younger people. Whether or not that proves to be the case will remain to be seen. A proposal might emerge from a group of single-person households with a common desire for a new CoHousing community together. What will not create a CoHousing community, however, will be if some people plan to set up a community on CoHousing lines, but to house others - i.e. not for themselves. Such an approach would dramatically fail to understand the key momentum in CoHousing development - that of households seeking to plan and satisfy their own household needs. It has already become an issue of concern in the US and the Netherlands where there have been some examples of housing developers building neighbourhoods marketed as suitable for a CoHousing identity to develop - this has not arrived after occupation, and muddles the super-ficial presentation of what CoHousing represents.

Even the OWCH group in London ,who may seem to be a selective background of people from one background - being only comprised of women - are from a range of ages and circumstances, and importantly their whole approach has come from the group's members themselves.

Summarising the distinctiveness of CoHousing neighbourhoods

The above contrast of CoHousing communities with similar-sounding 'communal living' or 'intentional community' arrangements in the UK should have already how CoHousing differs from those other initiatives. It will not, however, do any harm to restate CoHousing's core principles in order to underline its distinctiveness:

(i) CoHousing's combination of private and communal space

Readers of Diggers and Dreamers will be familiar with the record over some years of communities that have abundant common facilities and shared grounds. Many of the same set-tings, however, have seldom been able to offer all households or members fully self-contained accommodation, private to each household. Other co-operative groups, either have sep-arate households with self-contained dwellings or a collective shared property - what they do not have is both a self-con-tained privacy for member households, plus other shared facilities. The provision by CoHousing communities for their members to be completely private and to come together to share other activities, makes an important difference from those other places that might value such choice, yet do not have it in reality.

(ii) CoHousing's approach to designing for social interaction

CoHousing settings are designed to maximise 'intentional and incidental contact', a distinction from the customary layouts of UK housing areas which too often accentuate privacy at the cost of keeping neighbours separate from each other. CoHousing layouts deliberately site internal spaces where people spend a significant amount of time, like kitchen areas, towards outside communal spaces where neighbours might be, in order to bring about opportunities for residents to come into visual or verbal contact together. Parking areas and children's' play facilities are placed close to the 'common building' in order to encourage people to be naturally 'bumping into' each another - a clear distinction from how the placing of recreational facilities in conventional estate designs seems governed by an anxiety about disturbing the neighbourhood.

(iii) The CoHousing focus upon sustainable dynamics

CoHousing communities strike a balance between personal privacy and spending time with others that creates both a sense of intimacy and a shared common identity. This is supported by making the dimensions of the community of an appropriate size to sustain community relationships. A number of small group-living arrangements in the UK would not qualify as examples of CoHousing development because their numbers are too small a achieve a balanced 'sustainable dynamic'. Similarly, many wider housing estate areas would on their numbers alone (notwithstanding concerns about local decision-making, housing design, etc.) be considered too large to maintain the familiarity that is sufficient for a CoHousing identity. As Ward (1990) has noted, a crucial absence in modern housing estates that can number hundreds of dwellings is the chance to sustain a manageable group of neighbourly relationships.

If CoHousing has one key sustainable dynamic it is this attention given to be the scale of neighbourhood development. It should not be so small as to be over-powering in pressing households to interact constantly together, but neither too big as to be beyond sustaining meaningful contact and relationships with the other households in that neighbourhood.

(iv) The CoHousing emphasis on collective decision-making

The importance of equal contributions within modern collective decision-making arrangements like CoHousing is recognised as a fundamental aide to social cohesion. Fromm (1991, p.159) notes that *"in collaborative development, a sense of community appears long before the walls have been built and the legal papers signed"*. Formal structures may be required to facilitate key decision-making, however when people register that key decisions will rest with their own group then the time taken up by the planning and development of the community will strengthen a sharing of identity, rather than dissipate motivation. At key moments (like when new membership of the community up for discussion and transfers of accommodation could take place) it will be imperative that the community alone can determine how changes take place - not some absent property-owner or authority on the 'outside'. The shared opportunity to shape neighbourhood and neighbour relations will be a crucial contributor to a community's security and stability, and is a clear encouragement for members to identify one's own needs with those of the wider group.

Notions of sustainabilit', at least in the UK, do not usually include a focus upon community dynamics, and particularly not in the context of planning new neighbourhoods. CoHousing is not only focused very deliberately upon such dynamics but provides a clear model for evaluating the separate elements of neighbourhood plans and their interaction together. The importance that CoHousing gives to its scale of development, different from other approaches to 'communal living', is underscored by a real understanding of the difference this makes to the personal contact between the households of 'local' neighbourhoods, and how this difference underlies what turns neighbourhoods into communities.

The Community Project consists of over thirty adults and more than twenty children ranging in age from a few months to over seventy years old. Most of the group consists of families with one or more children, but there are also some couples and single people. Most adults are in their forties. A few of the group are retired, some are at home engaged in childcare, most have either full or part-time jobs. The skills in the group are wide-ranging, including managerial, artistic, teaching, computing, financial, to name but a few. Several work mainly from home, while a number work in the health, social services and voluntary sectors and others in the media and related areas.

In 1997 the Project purchased the site of a former small hospital situated on the edge of a small village in East Sussex. Members of the Project managed the entire process of converting the main part of the hospital buildings into seventeen individual homes. This ranged from overseeing the structural surveys, agreeing the architectural designs, obtaining planning permissions, tendering for building contractors and overseeing the actual conversion work.

Households had considerable input into the internal designs of their homes. The range of homes we have created are houses varying in size from two to five bedrooms, to different sized flats - all as home-ownership. We also own twenty-three acres of land, consisting of open meadowland, garden areas and woodland, plus a small pond that we would like to expand. All are shared communally.

A small number of other buildings on the site provide communal facilities for the group. One large building of 11,000ft, Shawfield, provides considerable communal facilities, including a hall, a large kitchen and dining area, meeting rooms, guestrooms and an office complex. This building is being gradually refurbished and decorated. Another building is still to be developed, and there is a workshop and tool pool in an old pump-house.

There is no one specific ideology that defines the Community Project. We maintain the privacy of family units by having individual housing, each with our own front door, though we aim as a group to live co-operatively as neighbours, engaging with each other in a number of social and practical ways to foster an enjoyable, supportive community environment. Whilst maintaining the privacy of individual homes, the aim of the group is to live co-operatively, jointly managing the land and communal facilities, informally sharing skills and support and generally enjoying each other's company. There is a desire to share resources where feasible and have a regard for ecological factors in our management of our facilities and land.

While we broadly share these ideals, we also value the variety of philosophies and lifestyles that individuals within the group aspire to. We do not feel that we have to like each other, although friendships inevitably develop, or agree with each other's points of view, but we aim to treat each other with respect and try to listen thoughtfully to each other's ideas.

While we wish to develop a strong sense of community within the Project, we have no desire to cut ourselves off from the wider world in any way. The nearby village has some six hundred inhabitants, a church, a primary school, a pub and a thriving village shop. A larger village, with a secondary school is just two miles away, and there are two small towns with train stations six miles away. The shop/ post office is twenty minutes walk, the school is half an hour's walk. There are three buses a day to the nearest town.

In summary, we are all keen on a spirit of community. We do not want an institutionalised feel, but we do want to be more than simply a housing estate. We want to live next door to people we know and trust, whose aspirations we share and can support and with whom we can work and play.

Getting started

The Community Project all started some 10 years ago, chatting over an Islington dining table about how life could be different if there was a greater sense of community between neighbours. One couple had a vision of a different type of communal and community lifestyle. After a number of years of doing some initial research and visiting other communities they shared their ideas with some friends and a small group of interested people formed, five of whom live at Laughton Lodge today. Now the chats take place over dining tables in rural Sussex and the participants can hardly believe that through years of hard work, determination and sheer bloody-mindedness, they actually made the dream into a reality!

It was envisaged that the project would consist of around 15 households, not least due to a feeling that the broader the size and the capital base, the greater could be the stability of the community. Below a certain size, community projects are vulnerable to the departure of any one member, and a small size of membership can too easily mean there is disproportionate pressure upon daily relationships.

It became apparent that it would not be possible for this small group to finance the purchase of a large enough property, so an advertisement was put in The Guardian property section seeking people to join them. Over seventy people responded and a few committed themselves to the project immediately. There were no entry qualifications : people selected themselves if they thought the ideas suited them. Over the course of the next five years people dropped out along the way, while others joined through personal contact or following the placing of a further advert and an entry in Diggers and Dreamers. Only about ten per cent of the total number of enquirers have actually stayed with the Project. It certainly took very much longer than anyone ever envisaged to move in to new homes and start to live as a community.

Maintaining momentum and participation
to develop the Community Project

There were a number of ways in which we maintained momentum during the project's long development and search for a suitable site. During the long time we were property-hunting, the group met monthly to talk about its philosophy, sort out legal issues and discuss ways of financing the project. Some of us went on frequent visits to see properties, which was exciting though often frustrating. It was important to have a hard core of very determined, - some would say obsessed - people who pursued new properties even when they were apparently unsuitable.

Much work was done in between meetings and during periods of 'high pressure'. A small executive team met weekly to manage the project's finer details, and to provide information for the main group. This larger group made all the big decisions, acting by consensus. It was agreed to have one main link person to liaise with each of the professionals in order to avoid duplication and confusion. These professionals included: estate agent, planning officer, solicitor, bank, structural engineer, architect, and building contractor.

The innumerable meetings were hard work but were often followed by a meal in a local cafe or by bringing food to share. We had a number of parties and a few residential weekends - heady occasions, which gave us a taste of what life together, might be like in the future. Occasional 'sharing the vision' exercises at meetings helped remind us of why we were involved. The enormous amount of work put in by some members of the group encouraged other more tentative members, and we attempted to nurture new members by telephone contact and encouraged them to take on specific jobs at an early stage. When the first family sold their house and moved into temporary rented accommodation in the area it made a big impact. The point at which people moved to new jobs in Sussex and the point when a few people put large sums of money into the project at an early stage - these steps demonstrated serious commitment and gave real encouragement to others. The day when we signed the forms to become Directors of the Company felt a very significant occasion. Such milestones helped us believe in the future even when progress was often agonisingly slow.

The regular subscription of ten ponds a month helped to reinforce the realisation that we were not merely a discussion group! More significant was the fact that members were required to make a deposit of ten thousand pounds once they were allocated a dwelling unit. If the member subsequently had to drop out they knew the deposit would not be returned until a new purchaser had been found and had replaced the deposit. This awesome step certainly concentrated the mind. Perhaps most important was the fact that it became virtually impossible to leave. After spending an increasing proportion of time involved in the project - in meetings, on the phone, or working alone at home on some aspect of the planning, time spent with other friends decreased. We got get closer and closer to each other. We had spent so much of our time planning, dreaming and discussing the project that we felt we couldn't leave. Inevitably some people did have to drop out though and it was agonising saying goodbye. We saw that it was a very difficult and painful thing to leave. We realised how lucky we were still to be able to remain in the project.

Keeping the group together became more important than finding a beautiful site in the right place. The power of the group became paramount. As this became apparent it was easier for us to compromise endlessly on things we had held dear - like the location and beauty of a building, delays and even cost.

Finding the property and securing approvals

It took three years to identify and acquire the appropriate property. There had been a number of unsuccessful attempts to purchase properties, and the group had found it particularly difficult to compete financially with property developers. Laughton Lodge was identified from information sought on the unwanted assets of statutory authorities, and had been a small rural hospital site.

The cost of converting the buildings into a sufficient number of homes turned out to be higher than originally expected and so the building of a few additional properties on the site proved necessary to make the overall project viable. In order to assist the overall financial position, members loaned as much as they could. Some had capital to contribute, while others raised money through increasing their mortgages, borrowing from friends and family or even selling their homes. These loans acted as down-payments towards their new homes in the Project. Some people put in more money than their home was likely to cost, and even with loan agreements in place people had to take considerable risks with all that they owned in order to secure the Project's finances.

By pooling their assets the group was able to purchase the Laughton Lodge site, but to undertake the conversion work (costing well over a million pounds) the backup of a loan agreement was essential to secure available funds, if they were required. Without a proven track record in property development, it took some time for the group to find sufficient funding that could cover the construction phase. Eventually Triodos Bank, which lends to 'social projects', agreed to provide a loan, although as it turned out we never needed to draw down any of those funds.

Obtaining planning permission for the conversion of the buildings and the building of four new homes ended up taking a year in itself. The local planning policy was to allow no new build in the area and so the new buildings were controversial. There was also local opposition to our plans, due to understandable suspicion as to exactly what this *community project* represented. A petition of over two hundred signatures was produced opposing the application. This made the overall process of obtaining planning permission even more tortuous and prolonged, and included intensive lobbying of the planning committee, presentations at meetings and a site tour for the Chair of that Committee. Planning permission was eventually granted and the group was ready to purchase the site, although there were a further few months of negotiation on the eventual price and then several more months of sorting out the tender for the building works.

The builders finally started the conversion of the buildings in 1998. As the building work progressed, members were starting to sell their homes elsewhere and although not done to a carefully organised plan, it so happened that as each phase of the work needed to be paid for, the Project had enough money to do so. Each family purchased their lease as their new home became ready, although the final prices were only worked out once the development phase was complete. Families started to move into their new homes in early 1999 - almost 3 years after Laughton Lodge had first been identified.

The final stage of the development has been the construction of the new houses. Households were recruited to the Community Project by the same process used for other members. These new members then bought their plots of land from the Project on a long lease (nine thousand, nine hundred and ninety-nine years), comparable to the leases for the refurbished units. The 'newbuild group' consulted closely with the rest of the community before plans for the houses were submitted to the local authority for approval, and the contractors could undertake the actual building work.

Daily life and 'consensus' decision-making

There are a number of ways in which the community meets and works together. Every Friday evening we have a pot-luck supper together in Shawfield, our communal building. It is a good opportunity to meet up and chat informally. It is quite unstructured and there is no pressure for households or members to attend. On an average evening between a third and a half of the community come along. Once a month we also have a 'work day', where we tackle outstanding tasks on the land or in the communal buildings. People choose which tasks they want to work on, and there is much camaraderie and rather long lunch-hours!

Perhaps most significantly of all, members of the Project meet in many, different, informal ways; for quick passing chats, longer chats over coffee, shared suppers, undertaking small projects in twos and threes, for an evening of music. Significant birthdays and events are often celebrated together and the seasonal calendar provides plenty of opportunities for parties. We support each other in many ways, looking after each others' children, lending a cup of sugar, being a listening ear, offering a lift to the station, helping to fix a leaking tap and so on. We try to pool resources as much as possible to minimise waste, and there is a tool pool, a laundry (although most households do have their own washing machines). We also buy a number of standard food and drink items in bulk at wholesale prices.

The Project's children have the kind of freedom to roam safely that is rare these days. They are often to be seen playing in groups, or travelling around the site on their bicycles. On fine days you can often spot a gang in the undergrowth during a complicated spying game and there are likely to be other groups in the tree house, or on swings or having scooter races. With twenty-three acres, a communal building and twenty-one houses to choose from, they are never short of somewhere to go, and they are in and out of each other's houses constantly.

All members are encouraged to belong to one or more sub-groups. These meet to discuss their work area in detail, although at the end of the day, individuals choose how much they wish to get involved in any events or other work for the community. Although none of the organised community activities are compulsory, individuals are expected to try to attend main group meetings and workdays. Inevitably there are always occasions when people cannot attend.

The sub-groups carry budgets, although large amounts of expenditure need to be ratified by the community's main group, which meets together in a more formal manner once a month. The agenda for the main meeting is circulated in advance, there are minutes taken and the meeting is chaired on a rotating basis. This is where major decisions are taken together about any aspect of our communal life and policy issues are aired and discussed.

All our decisions are made via consensus and it is fundamental to the way we operate. However it can be difficult and frustrating and we continue to struggle with how to make this effective. We do have a fall-back position in our guiding constitution [the Company's Memorandum and Articles of Association] allowing us to go to a vote if we cannot reach consensus after a set number of meetings, however we have yet to use it! And although we operate by consensus we also delegate to subgroups and give authority to groups and individuals for specific tasks and issues. This means we can avoid having to take every decision to a meeting of the whole community.

It is not easy for more than thirty adults to make decisions together. Meetings can be very lengthy when everyone wants their say and it can be difficult at times to resolve opposing views. Everyone, at one time or another, has had to let go of dearly held opinions, for the sake of finding some consensus with the wider group. While we strive to avoid any sense of institutionalisation, inevitably members may need to give up certain individual freedoms - for example, with no private land on the site, people need to negotiate before undertaking anything major in the garden areas. Compromise and negotiation remain the name of the game, although we are determined to improve our use of consensus decision-making to remove the tendency for current procedures to leave people feeling frustrated or sidelined. We remain committed to 'decision by consensus' despite knowing that we need to make it work better. This is because we know from other communities that other forms of democracy using majority voting mean people can become marginalised and excluded and this undermines group functioning.

Legal Structures and Finances

Legal structure

The Community Project is a Company 'limited by guarantee', set up with all appropriate legal documents (Memorandum, Articles of Association, leases, etc.). We were always keen to ensure that the Project was watertight from a legal point of view, and that the legal structure and documentation would ultimately provide recourse to the law if members did not meet fundamental obligations. We believed clarity in this area is crucial, although we are also aware that until any situation is put to the actual test it is difficult to know how watertight a document like our lease will turn out to be.

The Company owns the freehold of all the buildings and land on site. Members purchase individual properties from the Company by leasehold. All leaseholders are Directors of the Company, but they share in common with the other Directors the responsibility for the freehold of the site, including the land and communal buildings

All major decisions regarding the community are made by members at main group meetings, as noted above The main meeting is used for long term policies, strategic decisions and agreeing financial commitments. Most day-to-day decisions are made by sub-groups. These operate within a set budget and work plan for the following areas: new-build, maintenance, facilities, process, development, and land use.

Wherever possible, decisions are made by consensus. If required, the voting procedure we have as a fallback position stipulates that only Directors of the Company are eligible to vote. All names on the separate leases are Directors of the Company.

Finances

Members of the Project purchase their properties leasehold from the Company. It is left to each household to cover the costs of the lease in their own way. If mortgage finance is required it is assumed that members will obtain mortgages in the normal manner to cover their individual leasehold costs.

Members who wish to leave the Project will need to sell their leases. The terms of our lease agreements state that when an occupier wants to sell, the Company has three months to find a buyer at a price agreed between the Company and the vendor. This agreed price should incorporate an 'index linking' arrangement detailed in the lease which is designed to limit the sale price of outgoing members whilst enabling them to re-enter the external property market in a way comparable to living in an equivalent house in the village. If no-one is found in the three month period the vendor can then find their own buyer as long as the incoming household agrees to the terms of the lease and becomes a full member [i.e. Director] of the Company. It is likely that we may decide to extend the period of three months to six months in the future to allow the Company more time to find a suitable household that is keen to participate in the life of the community.

In order to maintain the land and buildings each household pays a monthly service charge (based roughly on the floor space of a household's dwelling - currently eighty-five pence per sq. foot. / per year). This sum is to be reviewed every year. An annual amount is also paid into a 'development fund' as agreed by the main meeting of the community.

Successes and Strengths

We are really just at the beginning of our community project. During the seven years of the "development phase" the group began to operate as a community together, but we recognise that we have much to learn about living together, making decisions together and achieving an appropriate balance between the needs of individuals and the needs of the group.

"Life here is characterised by caring support, friendliness, too many meetings, challenging disagreements, exciting and stimulating ideas and opportunities. It's exhausting and demanding but really enjoyable too. "

With the completion of the four newbuild houses, (which won an award for their 'eco' design), the main development phase is finally over. In terms of other practical plans, we have just completed an extensive participative exercise based on Planning For Real principles to look at how we should landscape and use our land.

Priorities stemming from that include establishing a kitchen garden, finishing landscaping the areas around the houses and undertaking a considerable amount of planting around the site, including an orchard. The common house, Shawfield, is gradually being refurbished, and its suite of eight offices for business use by members of the community is now functioning. The next priorities are improving the dining area, where we want to create a pleasant and welcoming space in which the community can meet and share a meal; setting up a children's room; and the development of guest rooms.

"Living with respect for diversity and individual private space, while at the same time having a commitment to the wellbeing of the group and the property we share. Sometimes I feel it is a challenge to balance my commitment to self, family, work and community but they are all an integral part of my life, and I consider myself very lucky to be part of this adventurous project."

We are now becoming integrated into village life. After initial suspicion from some people in the locality, Community Project members are now welcomed. We are represented on the local school governing board, on the village shop committee, and are beginning to play a significant part in the life of the village.

We are regularly contacted by individuals and groups all round the country and abroad for information and advice about how to start a CoHousing project. We have run some successful CoHousing workshops and we are greatly encouraged by the recognition given to what we have achieved.

"We should not underestimate how much we have learned to deal with different opinions. Many of us have made U-turns. While living in a 'me' centred society most of us learned how relative our own opinions are. I think these things have major effects on our identities. You learn to distinguish in a very short time what is important to you and what is not."

This is part of the challenge of living truly as a community, rather than a group of neighbours, and we expect that we will continue to develop as a group for many years to come.

"I remain unreconstructedly proud of the achievement of changing some knackered old hospital buildings into a decent place to live - a settlement that makes quite a considerable contribution to rethinking the ways in which people interact with their environment."

Ongoing Issues

We feel we have achieved a great deal and the uncertainties of the long development phase seem a distant memory. However, there are many aspects of community life which still need improvement.

Sustainability

Some ambitious hopes for recycling and environmental sustainability had to be dropped or at least delayed due to cost. Plans for solar heating, grey water recycling and a reedbed sewage system were dropped but may be revisited in the future. We do, however, have a district heating system using a woodchip burner with an oil boiler as a back-up. We have our own water supply from a borehole on-site, and our own telecommunications installation - an ISDN telephone and 'local area network', which means all internal calls are free. Decisions on double-glazing were made by members on a house-by-house basis. The location of our communal house, Shawfield, militates against some use of the communal facilities (like the laundry). Although we do not yet have a formal system of car pooling, a considerable amount of car sharing takes place informally and this is set to increase. There are management and work issues associated with some of the environmentally friendly elements of the project, such as the filling of the woodchip silo, although its tiring and messy nature has undoubtedly been a bonding experience for working together!

Keeping the site tidy

There tends to be a creeping accumulation of clutter in public spaces, both indoors and out. Our 23 acres are better looked after now than a year ago but junk still tends to gather outside and inside the common areas. We often blitz them on our workdays but they pile up again within a few weeks. Children's toys, remnants of encampments and bikes tend to be left around the site. We are still working on developing 'ground-rules' and arrangements for clearing up.

Sharing the work

Everyone is expected to try to attend monthly meetings of the main community group, monthly workdays and join at least one subgroup. Sometimes it appears as if some people are much more active than others. However, we have found that we can't and don't want to make community work compulsory. Also, it can be easy to overlook some forms of contribution and the changing pressures in peoples' lives means the time and energy available for the project fluctuates accordingly. At the end of the day, individuals choose how much they are prepared to do to maintain the life and fabric of the community.

Consensus and conflict

Although visitors and new members often complement us on the way we conduct meetings, we know we must find ways to improve the way we reach decisions. Being able to have robust discussions with opposing points of view without personalising issues, bullying, emotional blackmail or ridicule is something we are still struggling with.

'Conflict management' is one of the most difficult issues for the Project. We need to develop a forum for more exploration of feelings and vision. Without this conflicts can undermine other interactive processes. Most difficulties are about the relation between the individual and the wider community - which not surprisingly reflects a core conflict in society as a whole. Many conflicts in the Project arise from a tension between one's responsibility towards the group versus one's individual needs and motivations - for example, over personal use of land, personal responsibility for parts of land and negotiation with one's neighbours.

We currently use informal consensus decision making although we have experimented with a number of techniques. We have discussed the possibility of getting group training in the 'Formal Consensus' method.

Financial constraints

It is necessary to take individuals' financial circumstances into account when taking collective decisions about expenditure. We try to avoid putting people under pressure to agree to spend money while at the same time not hold back those who would like to spend more to improve the land or communal facilities. Further experience is needed in how to balance these factors.

Process for resale of units

When an occupier wants to sell, the Company has three months to find a buyer at a price agreed between the project and the vendor. This has proved rather short and we may decide to extend this to six months, although we are conscious that a longer period may have disadvantages too.

Use of email
The use of email within the Community Project has exploded over the last two years in common with the rest of the UK. Everyone is online. This saves time on meetings and telephone calls and is highly effective for information sharing. We have learnt however that it can be abused and that consultation via email has its dangers. It is recognised that sensitive matters need to be handled face to face and we are developing a local email etiquette.

More focus on interpersonal relationships
We want to develop ways of communicating feelings and sharing hopes and vision. Although there is some uncertainty about how best to approach this there is widespread recognition that greater understanding of each others core values and aspirations will deepen relationships and help us if or when conflicts arise.

Involving the children
We want to find ways of involving the children more fully in different projects and in communal work. This is so that they can exert more influence over the development of the community and share responsibility for looking after it.

Management of budgets and resources
We are still experimenting with the correct balance between responsible management versus too much bureaucracy.

Keeping the impetus
After all the hard grind and excitement of setting the Project up and moving in some of the excitement and closeness could disappear. Some are worried that we could lose the impetus and vision and end up just being good neighbours. This is something we are exploring.

Key Lessons Learnt

Do not underestimate the level of commitment required nor how long it takes to set up a CoHousing project. And do not underestimate how much work and time is needed from each member to keep it going.

A broad balance of ages, family structures and type of household might be desirable. It could be argued that households without young children - particularly single people and older people - are currently slightly less well catered for, as they are in the minority. More childless households, or households with older children, might lead to more community activities and organisational structures specifically designed around the interests of adults, older children or older people. However, it is recognised that any minority may feel somewhat disadvantaged. The overall aim should be to try to get a balance.

Everything takes time with more than 30 adults involved.

Recognise that the experience of living together may be quite different from how one would imagine it. Think carefully about how building and design will accommodate differing needs for privacy and communality, both indoors and out.

Dividing the cost of units into 'core' and 'extras' was a good process and may be useful for other groups. The 'core' cost was the cost of the shell and the 'extras' were everything on top of this including lighting, doors, built-in cupboards, double-glazing, etc. This allowed for varying financial circumstances of individuals - gold taps for the wealthy or from a boot sale for those on a tight budget!

Always remember that the best thing about "community" is the people and the worst thing about "community" - is the people.

Sarah Berger and Lucy Morgan-Jones are founder members of the Community Project. Both live on-site and, when other work permits, are active in supporting the development of new CoHousing communities elsewhere

Combining CoHousing and Co-operative

The CoHousing ideal represents the latest in a long line of models for intentional communities that have been influenced by the strong UK tradition of co-operative approaches to communal life. Certainly a number of CoHousing groups aspire towards being modern housing co-operatives in the hope that the explicit egalitarian values of a 'co-op' will exemplify the community that they consider a CoHousing development should provide.

This is often with an associated opinion that the essential 'shared' nature of a CoHousing development is something that ought to have an explicit co-operative ethos. At least one leading member of the UK Co-operative movement considers that the mixture of private and communal facilities in the CoHousing ideal is just what a 'good' co-operative ought to provide. By extension of this point, if Co-ops can already deliver the CoHousing ideal, he argued then that any initiative to promote the 'new' idea would be better spent promoting the flexible potential of more co-operatives! Yet, while it is certainly correct to highlight the collaborative natures of both CoHousing schemes and of housing 'co-operatives', it is not a foregone conclusion that aspirations to create either type of group will automatically result in the establishment of such communities. While it is important to plan for how egalitarianism could be established, it is also sensible to be aware of what can mitigate against the long-term development of a community into a mature equality.

The commentator that made reference to how existing co-operatives may already represent a CoHousing community went on to quote a 'co-op' body in South London that seemed to display all the necessary characteristics. The author of this work accordingly sought to contact the Co-op to see how they had developed their CoHousing character. The co-operative no longer existed! - that is to say, it was traced through one of its previous officers. It had developed as a series of houses for 'co-operative group living', with an impressive commitment to the sharing of key resources between members, including the pooling of car use and substantial income-sharing. It had only ever had, however, enough space to give its members sole privacy within their bedrooms : all other rooms and facilities were shared. Over time this contributed significantly to members choosing to live elsewhere, as the limited privacy and personal space proved too small for people to tolerate as a long-term housing or community solution. Members themselves ultimately closed that co-operative down.

What is illustrative of the above tale is not its reference to the perennial balancing act within 'intentional communities' between communal and private needs, and between community and private facilities. Neither is it an attempt to dismiss the integrity of the 'co-operative' framework. Rather, it is highlight the degree to which an element of confusion persists in understanding how the reality of 'co-operatives' in the UK should be related to contemporary aspirations for new 'intentional communities'. For groups interested in maximising the connection between CoHousing and 'co-operatives', it will help will be to clarify what CoHousing groups should address to secure an 'egalitarian' or 'co-operative' character. To some extent all the comments are inter-linked - 'egalitarian' principles will have a bearing upon membership, which will in turn underpin considerations of collective investments and how to marry this with individual ownership. Some attention has been given to the context of mixed-tenure developments, for this is a fundamental concern to CoHousing groups whose members come from a range of financial backgrounds, income levels, etc.

Principles for egalitarian CoHousing

When considering the basis on which Co-operative's have sought to structure & shape their guiding principles, and indeed from which much of the typical Model Rules have evolved over time, a number of key concerns are apparent:
(a) There is a requirement for upon a basic set of common aspirations within an equitable and democratic body, with a

clear formal framework of which all members will be aware.

(b)There is a commitment that any use of, and risk to, the body's resources - financial and otherwise - will be directed through a focus upon the advancement and betterment of all its members.

(c)There is an acknowledgement that working relationships between members can include both smooth and problematic times.

There are various summaries of 'guiding' principles for collective or communal-minded groups that CoHousing Groups could use as a first guide for their shared intention to create a new co-operative neighbourhood. Whatever a Group might choose, the ultimate purpose is to enable them to define their shared ambitions to new or prospective members in a way that allows for clear examination and a common appeal. Below are sketched the kind of principles used for such a purpose in the 'Statement on the Co-operative identity' from the International Co-operative Alliance.

The above principles summarise the concerns that a co-operatively minded CoHousing Group could use to map out its members' core values and common aspirations. Such principles can also be the basis on which other partners or individuals other than the CoHousing members (for example for project finances or investment) are able to relate their own relationship with the project.

Groups will need to be wary about setting up formal structures that will not be accountable to the members who will come to live in the CoHousing neighbourhood. Recognition of the importance in clarifying basic co-operative or collaborative principles during a Group's formative development period, and their application to proposals for a mixed-tenure development using private and public funding, has already been the basis of research carried out for the Older Women's CoHousing project in London .

Principles of 'intentional neighbourhoods' for CoHousing organisations

Definition

A CoHousing organisation is taken to mean an autonomous association of households united in their aspirations to meet shared residential and social needs within a jointly-owned and democratically-controlled intentional neighbourhood.

Values and Principles

[CoHousing] organisations are based on the values of social responsibility, democracy, equality, equity and solidarity, and on caring for others. CoHousing members will believe in the worth of a practical setting in which those values can be lived in practice. The following principles are guidelines by which CoHousing organisations can strive to put their values for intentional neighbourhood' into practice:

1st Principle: Neighbourhood membership .... open to all persons that come to live within the neighbourhood...

2nd Principle: Control by a democracy of members.... bodies to be controlled by all their members...

3rd Principle: Members and their economic participation.... members contribute to neighbourhood financial and social capital ...

4th Principle: Autonomy and independence.... organisations are autonomous, ... controlled by their members ....

5th Principle: Education, training and information...organisations provide education and training for all their members.

6th Principle: Co-operation among neighbourhoods... working together via local, national, and international contacts...

7th Principle: Concern for the neighbourhood community.... organisations sustain the development of their communities .....

[* With acknowledgement to the International Co-operative Alliance - 'Statement on the Co-operative identity']

Some issues to consider on egalitarian principles

The formal development of Co-op 'Model Rules' has been described as arriving at elaborate ways to set out what a community or organisation must do when 'things go wrong'. Certainly such sets of Rules put forward procedural action to take to deal with long-standing problems. One should not be too drawn, however, to think solely about formal procedures and thereby ignore what can be achievable by members' personal interaction(s). The first US CoHousing communities have not contemplated expelling members from their number if 'problems' arise, but have sought to address grievances by other personal interventions.

The first proposals from property developers to develop CoHousing-type projects are just beginning to appear in the UK. The character of these projects already involves key decisions being taken by the developer body - such as determining the size and density of units, and the level of communal facilities - rather than by the prospective CoHousing residents themselves. Experience from similar approaches to some CoHousing' schemes in the US and Holland has not been favourable, where this has been an impediment to how member-households develop a lasting and collective identity together. At times there has also been a reluctance by developer-bodies to remove themselves from the scheme - It is a complaint from some Older Peoples schemes in Holland that it is still their Housing Association who takes key decisions on future membership and residency, rather than the CoHousing body itself.

It could be argued that a Group like the Older Women's CoHousing project in London could not be a co-operative body, as it is only open to women and is not open to 'all'. This would be a criticism that misses the crucial point of why some groups of individuals or households come together in the first place - namely because of a common experience and identification with a distinct social circumstance. There is nothing in the formal requirements for legal incorporation in the UK that would prevent a single-sex group from operating or registering as a co-operative.

At least one UK Group has been considering that members might provide different levels of personal investment into the project, and then be permitted to have more 'say' within the formal decision-making structure, in relation to their input to the project's development finance. Such a system would not seem to mirror the spirit of 'equality' enshrined in the history of co-operative bodies, and it could be thought would leave a legacy for a distinct imbalance in the community in the future. Where a project might consider it to be expedient that individuals offer additional financial resources than the minimum, Groups should consider how to direct that investment into the collective organisation (for example as form of 'loan stock', with some agreement for financial returns). Differences in individual investment in CoHousing property should still try to minimise disparity between what members are worth to the community. Any investment should also not be linked to more than a single residence, in order that the community is not faced with additional problems if or when the investing household come to redeem their stake.

Formalities and membership

The legal and financial structure(s) suitable for the formal establishment and governance of 'co-operatives' in the UK have been used for a multitude of different, collective, business and management ventures. All are nowadays registered as a particular type of legal body - an Industrial and Provident Society - which is a formal category of benevolent society that lays down the legal parameters for the acceptable roles, responsibilities and benefits of its members, set up for mutual benefit.

The formal operation of Industrial and Provident Societies are governed by sets of very formal rules. Over time the regulatory authority (now a part of the Financial Services Agency FSA) has given some of these sets of rules the status of - Model Rules, which lay out the precise legal structure and conditions for the governance of different kinds of 'I&PS' bodies. Such 'Rules' have been compiled and developed over the years into a repository of all that is classic to the 'co-operative ethic':

- each society must act and operate transparently democratically;
- each must accept that all members will have equal rights and equal responsibilities in the afford of the organisation (although some members are appointed to titular positions within the organisation to see its operations are conducted on a day-to-day basis on behalf of the whole membership body);
- each individual member has an equal stake to voting in his or her co-op's decision-making structure;
- each member is able to claim an equal portion of the benefits that are attendant to being a member of the co-operative (such as the right to live in a prop erty provided by the co-op).

A formal membership to such a body is assigned to individual members through the issue of a nominal 'share' in the co-operative. Such 'shares' are not tradable commodities, and are not the same as shares that are bought and sold on the Stock Exchange. Rather, they indicate that (a) each individual member has an equal 'share' or stake in the responsibilities and duties that the 'co-operative' sets upon all members; and (b) that this readiness to share in the responsibilities and duties brings a limit to the degree of each member's personal liability for the co-operative activities, that might arise from its subsequent operations or engagements with the world at large. An acceptance of some limit to one's personal or individual benefit is thereby balanced by a corresponding limit on personal liability - subject to the operations of the organisation having been conducted competently and in 'good faith' (i.e. not fraudulently).

The development of co-operative organisations and enterprises has been assisted in the UK over many years by a broad and expert body of support that has grown up to help 'co-ops' develop their business and management competencies. It is a wide body of support that is committed to offering advice and training to co-op bodies, and at times to offer financial assistance, such as 'business loans'. There is also a clear commitment to seeing 'co-operatives' develop sustainable futures for themselves. The recent development of a new set of Model Rules for a CoHousing Co-operative sponsored by an active co-op support agency, is specifically in response to the interest in combining CoHousing with the ethos and operation of a 'co-operative' organisation.

Some Issues to consider on Membership

Examples of legal structures are given in the Part Three of this publication. These include the Model Rules for a CoHousing Co-operative, alongside outlines of other UK organisational structures which can also demonstrate a responsibility or focus towards promoting a 'common benefit'. It is not the case that only a 'co-operative' structure provides an 'egalitarian' one : for example, this can also be achieved through a 'Company Limited by Guarantee' structure, which includes many of the aspirations and community-minded safeguards of the classic co-op body.

The formal and legal structure of a 'co-operative' can be used for property-owning, or for property management, or for a combination of ownership and collective tasks. A single CoHousing Group could also have more than one formal identity - it could be a co-operative as well as register as a 'imited Company (or even as a charitable body). Different registrations can provide the means for achieving different but complimentary aims.

It might be argued that a corporate body (like a Housing Association) should be part of the formal membership of a CoHousing project, by virtue of them providing finance towards one or more of the properties. Groups will need to decide whether or not to permit such organisational bodies to have exactly the same kind of long-term membership as individual household members, such as that provided under rules for 'co-operative' membership. Even where a property has a charge being held over it by a finance body [by way of being insurance for non-payment of the initial loan], this charge will not exist for all time. It will finish when the mortgage or loan is redeemed. There can therefore be some

Thinking About CoHousing

natural reluctance to giving finance bodies a full membership equal to the resident households, when their finance will only be required for a fixed period! If a CoHousing project can only proceed with some degree of corporate partners, it may be that Groups keen on a 'co-operative' registration will need to consider a separate formal partnership basis for how the collected CoHousing households collaborate with their institutional partner(s.)

While it can be acknowledged that a number of the European CoHousing communities have evolved from a clear 'co-background, it should not be assumed that this can provide sufficient parallels to subsequent CoHousing development in the UK. Countries such as Denmark and Holland have retained a practical and financial support for the choice of 'co-operative' tenure within their respective housing markets that is not the same for the position of co-operative housing in the UK. The ethos of co-ops in all these countries is certainly comparable, however the opportunities for co-op development within them are much less similar.

Property tenures and investment

The historical involvement of UK housing co-operatives and their support organisations has been almost exclusively to focus upon the provision of accommodation for rental tenure alone. This has been both because rental bodies have made no requirement for any degree of personal investment - it is the collective body that has sought the resources to create the accommodation - and to maintain property solely in the co-operative ownership of the collectively-managed organisation. In a few settings the body of membership of some co-operatives has come to include leaseholders (i.e. owners) alongside a majority of a rental tenure - principally where 'co-ops' have acquired property with prior-established leasehold residents. A few intentional community settings have mixed a collective ownership of property with selling some of the individual spaces to member households (such as at the Old Hall community in Essex).

Alongside this key characteristic that co-ops predominantly provide properties to rent, are the variations amongst individual housing co-operative properties. Some housing co-operatives are able to provide self-contained dwellings for all member households. Some, however, have only had a property separated into private or semi-private areas, thereby requiring all within the property to a sharing of basic amenities and washing and cooking facilities.

The interest from some UK CoHousing groups to combine the ideological background of collective and communal ownership with a more personal and individualised element of 'property equity' is therefore not immediately comparable the 'co-operative' property that has existed beforehand, and has little precedent within current 'housing co-operatives'. There has furthermore been a clear intention throughout much of the co-operative movement's history to limit individual ownership by co-operative members in the co-operative's business. This has been as much from an explicit value in prioritising the worth of collective ownership, and seeking to ensure that monetary value of the Co-op can benefit all members, as from seeking to minimise the potential for friction between individual self-interest and wider concerns for the collective good. The new set of Model Rules for registration of CoHousing Co-operatives is in part a recognition that attitudes to property ownership have changed, but that this could still be accommodated within an overall membership of a mix of 'owners' and 'renters' (or even part owners/part renters). It may be argued, however, that a prevalent attitude towards property 'investment' in the UK will consider it quite acceptable to prioritise the safeguarding of individual's investments above other considerations. Certainly it is not inevitable for Groups to come to conflict between combining the values of a shared-living community with opportunities for some personal ownership of the CoHousing property! What will always be more important for the community is the commitment and resources to build up the spirit of such a neighbourhood - this is clearly not solely of a financial nature, and the real energies put into the task are not directed towards monetary values.

Groups that aspire to mixed-tenure neighbourhoods will certainly need to be imaginative and understanding about what the actual number and mix of such tenures might entail. Anxiety about this could be eased through a positive evaluation and focus upon each individual's commitment to the community being considered of the greatest benefit to the neighbourhood, rather than the financial worth of any tenure or property investment on which their household occupies a property. There may always be a monetary difference between the shared goals of a collective enterprise and the value of any individualised receipt (such as a financial dividend that people might receive in common with at least some others). Yet even where 'property-ownership' is to occur, the worth of initial differences between households can be held in proper perspective. The income from a member-household paying rent in a mixed-tenure development may be as essential to the overall scheme's economics as the funds from ownership households. The renter-member could also be given the opportunity to 'own' a percentage of their property in the future (or receive a small sum on leaving their property), when their rental income has proved to cover its share of the original development finance.

In some CoHousing communities agreed mechanisms are in place to put limits or 'ceilings' to the prices at which individually 'owned' property is sold. This has been in order to prevent future property sales from spiralling to such heights within the property market that it deters or prevents would-be members from joining those communities. One mechanism used is to limit price rises to only a nominal cost-of-living increase. Another arrangement is to link property sales to a local index of property market levels, or to independent property evaluation (although this could be a less reliable means of achieving the goal of keeping prices down to a level of cost that will be 'affordable' to people wishing to join a CoHousing community for what it is, and more than merely a pleasant place to reside).

Time will tell whether or not people attracted to CoHousing projects in the UK who come with rigid thinking about some absolute importance of their property investment, rather than a flexible readiness to explore and prioritise a more collective property-ownership based upon a communal investment. In practice, a trust in a common and willing commitment to the community should mean, by default, a minimal level of decisions that would deliberately weaken the collective community. If no decisions come forward that deliberately weaken that community spirit, one would hope that by extension there will be no serious jeopardy to the value of the financial investment bound up in members' property. The surest security to CoHousing property investment will be the degree in which it is considered to be a thriving and successful community neighbourhood. It is therefore a testament to both the CoHousing ideal and to many established CoHousing communities that their success is demonstrated in financial terms, namely in the strength of their property sales and values when re-sales or transfers occur!

Some Issues to consider on Property Tenure and Investment

It will be prudent for CoHousing groups to acquire the site on which to develop their community with a 'freehold' ownership to its legal title. This will mean that the Group could retain a 'collective' freehold ownership when releasing any property on the CoHousing site to community members on the basis of a lease (for ownership or for rent). Holding the freehold title in its own right would mean that the group should be able to determine how it plans to use the site or overall property without undue deference to others. Releasing units only on a leasehold basis would allow the community to put requirements or covenants within the terms of such lease that are designed to strengthen the community setting.

For some property acquired on a leasehold basis in the UK, the leaseholder may have the legal right to buy the entire freehold at some unspecified future date. Conditions apply as to the type of property and to the length of lease to which this legal right applies. It is acceptable, however, that property developed specifically within the intention of providing a 'community' character can be exempt from such legislative permission, and CoHousing groups could look at establishing their members' future rights and limits with that in mind. Groups will certainly need to consider whether or not they would wish to have some of their neighbourhood property held in 'outright' ownership by individual property-owners in the future (i.e. that a leaseholde' has become a freeholder), or have all the freehold title retained in perpetuity by the collective body.

Households who already have the resources or income to embark upon property ownership could plan to be part of a membership of a CoHousing Group based solely upon an 'ownership' tenure (should one exist). It is not the same for households without the resources to be property owners - they could have to leave a Group that had settled upon an 'ownership' scheme, or be unable to join such a Group in the first place. Almost all UK Groups have households with access to resources that could be used in a CoHousing 'ownership' project. Most Groups, however, are a mixture of households with some resources (e.g. an existing mortgage or savings) and households without, and juggle with ideas about a single project that could provide a mixture of properties for owners and renters. Notwithstanding how this may be achieved, it is always open to a Group to assist its households to have at least a small 'ownership' stake in the project in the future. The Group could transfer a nominal percentage of a project's equity in the rental properties directly to those households that pay rent. This could be increased in the future if the household buys additional equity, if or when the household has the resources available.

Similar to the point raised under above, support for a CoHousing scheme from corporate or institutional finance, such as through a Housing Association, may require that body to have some form of a tenure stake in part of the CoHousing property. A CoHousing group may have little alternative than accepting this requirement, for example that a Housing Association 'owns' the lease of the properties that are for rent. The Group could, however, negotiate the terms of the property investment by that body so that conditions apply such that this will not weaken or undo the community's collective well-being. Such negotiation should also look to minimise the time within which that third party organisation has any formal interest in the community's property, and agree how the household or the community as a whole could acquire the property at some future time.

In terms of how CoHousing households may wish to make use of their individual homes, the possibility of any potential sub-letting of CoHousing units requires careful consideration. A number of the US communities quickly found that 'sub-letters' were more prominent in the neighbourhood than the original household, yet the sub-letters had no formal status (or obligations) as real 'members' of the community. It is worth noting that within various models of UK co-ops, where a tenant does not occupy their property for more than a stated period, they are liable to lose their membership in the organisation and thereby their right to reside in the property. Such a rule might not be so straightforward with leaseholders of owned property, however a community could set a condition in leases that sub-letting may only happen with the permission of the community body, or for minimal periods. It could be ensured that this is not solely to individuals independently letting out all or part of their property.

There have been a number of recent initiatives implemented in the UK designed to assist people to 'buy' the property in which they reside, rent, or have by lease. (Even leasehold-ownership usually do not immediately provide outright ownership - the freehold element is owned by the freeholder.) For CoHousing communities, Right to Buy issues will be as important as considerations about what rights or opportunities property-owners should have when they wish 'to sell'. Property being sold to new households that have no interest in joining-in with the community - i.e. taking part in shared or communal activity - will not be a sufficiently advantageous transfer of property rights, and they could be disastrous for the community dynamic of the remaining membership. It will not be a positive development if each new incoming household is not just as committed to being part of the community neighbourhood as all the original members. On the other hand, members may have to move away for a number of reasons, and it will not be advantageous to them to be forever restricted in how they can be released from their CoHousing property. It may be a little drastic to stipulate that a whole scheme should be put up for auction if one owner cannot be found a buyer in a few months - as agreed by one UK group! What will be of key importance in practice is the degree of compromise agreed by a group to release a member's equity or finance, in a way that can still assist the community to identify new member-households who genuinely want to join a CoHousing neighbourhood.

It should hopefully be clear from the above points that the respective values of CoHousing Groups and Co-operative bodies are not at all mutually exclusive. Indeed there are many ways in which the intentions of being a 'co-operative' can reinforce the collective aspirations to create a mutually supportive CoHousing neighbourhood. New approaches to co-operative operations are being developed, including the new tenure of 'Commonhold'. It will be interesting to see what future these may have for CoHousing aspirations.

Where UK CoHousing projects and traditional co-operative ideals may look at community interaction through different perspectives is principally in the context of property investments, for this has certainly not been a salient feature of UK co-operative life. A number of points have been raised to act as prompts to Groups to review their assumptions about financial investments, and contrast these against an investment in principles focused upon a non-monetary benefit to all members of their schemes, regardless of any differences in personal finances.

CoHousing communities for older people
Maria Brenton

This chapter looks at CoHousing Communities for people over fifty who choose to live with their age-peers. Such communities have a special value for older people in terms of continued social interaction, security, personal autonomy, self-governance and mutual support. The ageing of society, where a growing proportion of the population will be aged 50 years and over confronts us with a challenge we have not yet recognized fully. Meeting this challenge is especially imperative in relation to the built environment and housing where barriers to a healthy and sociable ageing prevail. CoHousing offers a model for discussion that links social relationships and design and can act as an antidote to such barriers, offering an imaginative option for older people who want to stay independent.

Older People and CoHousing

CoHousing, as a form of intentional community, offers a formula that many people will find attractive if the cultural and institutional barriers to it happening in Britain can be surmounted. The term CoHousing, coined by American architects, McCamant and Durrett, (1994) has come to stand for a combination of features originally designed in Denmark by young families and single parents for their own social needs. Equally, CoHousing offers to older people a positive blend of separate and independent living in a social and neighbourly environment. Developing a CoHousing Community is about collaborative living. It is more than a housing complex? it is a way of life which aims to stimulate neighbourly links in a specific neighbourhood and its physical design enhances this. Its main elements have been identified by Fromm (1991) as a mix of common facilities, private dwellings, resident structured routines, resident management, design for social contact, resident participation in the development process and pragmatic social objectives.

Being involved with and supported by people in one's neighbourhood, enjoying accommodation designed for easy social interaction and having a common space in which to meet and share activities are all features of CoHousing which are important for any age group. These features are particularly important, however, to people who are tied to a particular neighbourhood in a special way because their day-to-day lives are home-based. When you are old and are no longer in employment or have finished raising a family, you tend to be home-centred - often by choice but sometimes from necessity. Unless you live in an extended family, then friends and friendly neighbours assume an even greater importance than at earlier stages of your life.

In Western society, while early old age is for many people a time when they can positively blossom and explore new activities and challenges, free of the responsibilities they used to carry, it is also a time when social connections can begin to diminish. Work links fade; children and grandchildren move away; divorce may leave people alone and single again; friends and partners die one by one as your generation gets older. For most women, especially, extreme old age means a life lived alone. If you have slowed down physically, become less mobile or more frail, then you have all the more need of familiar support and companions in your own immediate neighbourhood. If it is the case that you have lived in your locality for a long time, you may have those supports in place. On the other hand, the locality may have changed around you and you may not know anyone any longer. Older people have a special need to re-create through a CoHousing Community a neighbourliness that has got lost in the rapid pace of change.

The advantages of living with other older people

Most literature and debate on CoHousing focuses on a family model whereby parents with children cluster together to form something like a small hamlet where cars are kept outside, children can play safely and adults can meet easily. Single adults of all ages and childless couples are also incorporated but the dominant model is a family one, particularly in the United States. In Denmark, the Netherlands and Germany, however, this model co-exists with one developed by and for people over 50. In these countries, older people have a choice to become part of an inter-generational CoHousing Community but many choose to form a community with their peers.

Ask residents in the nearly 200 CoHousing Communities of older people in the Netherlands why it is that they have elected to live only with their age peers, they will answer along the lines of *"We love our grandchildren. We like them to visit. We are also glad when they go home!"* They also point out that the age range of their communities - from around 55 to 90+ years old - embraces much diversity, stimulus and interest even though the outside world may regard them disparagingly as "old age ghettos". They offer a combination often of quiet peacefulness when you want it at night along with a connectedness and sociability during the daylight hours that might not be so readily come by in an inter-generational environment dominated by families. Their members may recall long, quiet days of feeling isolated and at risk in deserted suburbs where neighbouring families were out at work or school all day. Now they have neighbours who share the same time clock and pattern of activities as they, who don't skateboard in the hallways and don't play loud music into the early hours.

The greatest value of CoHousing for older people lies in the ready availability nearby of companionship and social activity. Contrast this with the life lived by many older people where they may not see or talk with another person for days or where their contacts with relatives or care agency workers are limited to service delivery or quick safety checks. In a setting where you and others have consciously chosen to be neighbours, there is a reciprocity which validates you as a social being. You are there on the same basis as the others and they can expect from you what you expect from them. The group may or may not organize formal activities such as shared meals, but casual friendliness and a willingness to help are taken for granted. The difference between this and available forms of residential care or sheltered housing, is not only that you and the group control your environment but that some care has gone into ensuring that there is a level of common interest and compatibility among you - which gives a more natural basis for reciprocity.

Prevailing choices in the UK

Choice of purpose-built accommodation for older people in the UK is not a current priority for bodies involved in new housing provision. The increasing mismatch between the needs of ageing individuals and the housing they occupy, and between demographic trends and housing supply, is a presenting symptom of rigidities in British society deriving partly from the inherent conservatism of our construction industry and our social and financial institutions. These are mostly still fixated on the production of uniform, privatised boxes for a social unit that has changed significantly in my lifetime ? the nuclear family. This accommodation is generally too large for the single ageing individual and is often not amenable to reconfiguration for unrelated singles to share its use. The technology is available(Gann 1999)to build flexible homes which can be easily adapted for a change of use or for a smaller household unit but imagination and social will are lacking and resources are therefore limited.

Some purpose-built accommodation for older people does exist in the UK, in the form of sheltered housing. It might be argued that CoHousing has therefore already arrived for older people. In sheltered housing they may each have their own private, self?contained space and share a common lounge, often with a kitchen, sometimes with a guestroom. This form of housing can offer an alternative preferable to isolation in a large, inconvenient house. Space-wise, however, the mean spatial standards of much specialist accommodation for older people in Britain can act as a deterrent to people wishing to size down to a more comfortable level. More to the point, as becomes clear later in this chapter, sheltered housing does not manifest the essential characteristics of CoHousing - which are consumer choice, familiarity with neighbours, intentional community (and so, values in common) and control of your environment. In sheltered housing, it is an external body (housing association, local authority, commercial company) which develops and usually manages the scheme. Developing the building precedes allocation of tenancies or sale, so there is no opportunity for a group to form and get to know each other in advance. The residents are strangers who have in common only their age and need for support and security. From this unpromising start, it is perfectly possible for neighbourliness and a sense of community to develop over time ? particularly if there is an active manager on site to stimulate it ? and for residents to enjoy a happy, socially connected life together. On the other hand, the general lack of use of their common rooms may confirm that sheltered housing does not automatically generate a sense of community or group dynamism.

The purpose?built housing options on offer in Britain to meet the needs of rising numbers of older people are distinctly limited in supply and there is little sign that we are getting 'ahead of the game' in the face of this challenge. The living space we deem appropriate for older people can often isolate them just as much as lack of integration with a neighbourhood and transport links. Older people spend much more time in their homes than other age groups and need space for separate sleeping arrangements, entertaining guests or enjoying hobbies. Housing should be more than somewhere to live. It is a key element in the maintenance of health and social connectedness - as we have noted, a dimension particularly important to people whose social networks shrink as they get older. One major trend we need to recognize is household fragmentation and the shift towards the single householder. The Housing Green Paper (DETR 2000) notes the projected rise in single householders, but comments, 'this is not always reflected in the variety of homes being provided to meet the needs of the future.' Single occupancy is a feature of life in late age - especially for older women. Under-occupied large houses, low incomes and a dearth of imaginative and acceptable alternative housing forms combine to reduce their choices and constrain their lives. Design of new models or more help with reconfiguring existing accommodation could help single people to live in a way that also acknowledges and addresses social needs.

Dutch CoHousing communities of older people

Developments in Denmark and the Netherlands have offered a model for the Older Women's CoHousing project - which will be the first of its kind in Britain to be set up by older people. CoHousing has become an accepted option for older Dutch people over the last 10 to 20 years. Typically, a small group of older people will take the initiative to gather around them other interested individuals to plan and develop a residential community which they will themselves run. In the Netherlands, (Brenton 1998) most groups have enlisted the help of a housing association and a local authority in finding land and identifying finance. In the past, they have been developed within the social housing sector, which is larger and more generous than its British equivalent. In recent years, however, cost constraints have stimulated a mix of owners and renters. There are nearly 200 actual and intending CoHousing Communities of older people in the Netherlands with an average age of around 70 years (Vrom, 1998). From a public policy point of view, they are seen as a valuable social investment in the well?being and independence of older people and a means of reducing or at least delaying demand for health and social care support services. In recent years, the development of CoHousing Communities out of existing residents of blocks of flats has gained policy attention. This is known in the USA as 'retrofit CoHousing' where the social relations are 'retrofitted' rather than the structures.

Finance of the development in the Dutch social housing sector of CoHousing communities of older people has been the responsibility of housing organizations which have until recent years been funded directly from the public purse. Nowadays, they are self?standing in the market and do not receive government subsidies. They do, on the other hand, benefit from cheap capital loans backed by government guarantee. Dutch housing, less viewed as an investment commodity than is the case in Britain, has traditionally been biased towards renting, although this is changing. There is a high degree of regulation in the housing sector, the 'Delft' model of consumer choice prevails (and is being tested in Britain) and individual rent subsidies are available to meet housing costs.

Design for social connectedness

In terms of physical design and amenity, the quality of these Dutch CoHousing developments is striking. Four dimensions merit special mention: domestic space; communal space; design for interaction and integration with the neighbourhood.

In a country that enjoys the distinction of being the most congested in Europe, space standards for modern specialist housing for older people in The Netherlands would and should put British housing providers to shame. In British social housing, prevailing space norms in social housing for a person over the age of 55 years are 37- 45m 2 which allows of one bedroom. Private sector developers try to impose even less space than this. In the Netherlands, allocations for occupants in this age group are anything from 70m2 from the 1970s era to 80m2 - 90m2 or even larger nowadays. The Dutch housing association de Woonplaats, an agency specializing in the provision of accommodation for older people, specifies on its web?page a minimum space allocation of 80m2 for new developments. The Dutch Government has acknowledged officially that older people will no longer accept only one bedroom and that two bedrooms should become the norm (Vrom 1997). Such comparatively generous space allocations allow for an extra room for a hobby or for accommodating relatives, friends and helpers. Often there is the possibility of a flexible use of space. Some Dutch senior CoHousing developments have the capacity for easy removal of a wall to enlarge living space or to provide a hobby or computer area in an apartment. Such a facility may be provided in addition to that of common guestroom(s) and a common lounge and kitchen as well as a garden. The apartments are built to a 'barrier?free' design, without thresholds, with wide doorways and with wheelchair accessible rooms and bathrooms.

CoHousing groups of Dutch older people also often take part in determining the design of their accommodation, facilitated by architects and developers who believe in consumer participation. A group of around 44 people aged up to their late eighties in Amersfoort celebrated their tenth anniversary in 2000 as a co?residential group. In the mid 1980s, when they were meeting to develop their aims, they designed their own flats with an architect who advised them within a cost envelope. The final stage of their participation was to visit the construction studies department of a local university to 'build' their own apartment in polystyrene blocks. Their two buildings are designed around a large garden of their own making, with front doors and galleries facing each other across it, and are connected by a bridge and lift tower that serves both buildings. The small car park is on the periphery. What they like about the design is the ease with which they meet each other casually - while preserving their own privacy and personal space. They also live five minutes walk from a small village shopping centre.

Developers of new buildings in The Netherlands are encouraged also to conform to the Dutch ideal standard or 'keurmerk' of housing for older people and new general housing, which awards recognition for design and for features which integrate a development into its neighbourhood. The criteria for this senior chartermark, judged in the case of older people's dwellings by a local older people's committee, include proximity to local shops and transport routes, accessibility and size, security and flexibility for changing needs. These standards plus provisions like common rooms etc. are a feature of much of modem Dutch provision for older people ? not just of CoHousing communities.

Common interests

All being 'old' together is not a sufficient basis for people to develop a thriving group life. There has to be more to it. A basic minimum of shared values and common interests is needed as a unifier - as a reason for putting energy and commitment into building a sense of group solidarity and sharing activities. This doesn't mean uniformity - far from it. The diversity of a group is also important where individuals can bring varied life experiences, skills and resources to keep things lively. 'Community of interest' is an essential contributor to developing the 'community of place' that older people have special need of. It is helpful also to have other links between individuals in the group such as religious background, ethnic culture, professional identity, an interest in rambling or gardening or painting or a mix of all these and others. Shared interests may be found by happy accident in settings like sheltered housing, where strangers are put together on the basis of age. In CoHousing, a basic community of interest is part of its design and purpose, at the very least in relation to subscribing to the shared life of the group. It is and should be a defining criterion for entry to the group because this is what makes it different from other kinds of group living.

Security and mutual support

For older people who live alone, having the security of attentive neighbours who will notice if you don't appear one morning is very important. Alarm systems may supplement such a resource but can never satisfactorily replace it. A commitment to mutual support, where members of the group offer each other the assurance of short-term and emergency help and care is a prominent feature of older people's CoHousing Communities, precisely because some of their members are at an age where it may be necessary. Care needs to be taken that groups maintain an age range that is wide enough to remain attractive to new members, to sustain reciprocal services and to ensure a natural renewal process.

Where CoHousing communities in the social rented sector are concerned, Dutch local authorities and housing association landlords have long conceded to their tenants the right to allocate vacant tenancies. The CoHousing group, with its accent on mutual support and shared activities, can only succeed if its members share commitment and values and a certain compatibility. For older people living closely and inter-dependently in a mutual support system, this is even more important. Accordingly, with specific safeguards in relation to the costs and lengths of voids, the groups maintain their own waiting lists based on their own selection criteria.

Autonomy

The autonomy and self-governance enjoyed by CoHousing Community residents is especially important to those who are approaching old age now - those who are in their late fifties and early sixties who are from a modern gen-eration that has known more freedom and self-expression than its predecessors. Institutional care is not attractive to them. In my research in the Netherlands (Brenton 1998), group members said to me 'Here I can make up my own mind. There is no-one telling me what to do - and I have all the benefits of group living into the bargain'. Being in a community of one's peers can make a difference - studies of the co-operative housing movement over the years have indicated that older members can feel disempowered and excluded by the domi-nant and sometimes conflicting interests of families with chil-dren. Older people's concern with autonomy and independ-ence is stronger in countries like the Netherlands and Denmark than in the UK, where the older population is less politicised and organised and where paternalism and a dependency culture predominate in housing and welfare serv-ices. The culture and history of those societies is also more geared to collective approaches to individual and social needs. I have argued, however, (op cit 1998) that the post-war baby boomers who are the coming generation of older people in Britain are likely to reject the limited options currently open to older people in Britain. Already many view with dismay the possibility of facing an old age in sheltered housing or in old people's homes - or, more likely, that of remaining isolated and unsupported in their own homes. They may come to CoHousing ten or twenty years after their peers on the Continent but once they have recognised its value as a posi-tive and alternative way of supporting the ageing process, there will be demand for it as the baby boomers grow old.

The UK's Older Women's CoHousing Project

The Social Housing sector in Britain has not yet been tested by the demands of CoHousing which is not a familiar mode of collaborative living in Britain. There are very few examples of a CoHousing Community in this country; and those that exist are based on families and single people of a range of ages - none is designated for people over fifty years of age. It is likely that the first such community will be one piloted by the Older Women's CoHousing (OWCH) group in London, cited within the Government's strategic framework for older people's housing (DETR./DH 2001) looking at new policy and service developments for older people.

The OWCH project is a pilot scheme that has attracted support and interest from the Joseph Rowntree Foundation and from the Housing Corporation. It has been in existence since mid-1998 and was started by a small group of women aged from their late fifties to early seventies. In a capital city where 78% of people over 60 years living alone are women, these women all live alone and are keen to develop a collaborative way of living on one site in London. They want self-contained accommodation but to share common space and activities and offer each other support as they grow older. They have chosen to develop a women-only CoHousing Community which will welcome women over fifty who are prepared to commit themselves to the group's values of participation and mutual support, respect for diversity and a non-hierarchical way of operating. They are keen to continue developing their own skills and personal growth, to counter ageist stereotypes and to make a contribution to the wider community. They also want to pioneer their CoHousing Community as a model which can be replicated by other groups of older people.

Members of the OWCH group visited several Dutch CoHousing Communities of older people to draw on their experience in developing CoHousing. Arising from this visit, the video 'A Different Way of Living' was later filmed featuring four of the Dutch groups and the OWCH group in London, as an educational and promotional tool for the group. What also emerged was an interest in a future international holiday exchange system between CoHousing Communities of older people.

The OWCH group, which became a Company Limited by Guarantee in 2002, will manage their future project themselves with a Registered Social Landlord (RSL) acting as a managing agent. The mixed tenure nature of the project is of great interest to the Housing Corporation which has funded an Innovation and Good Practice Study into the legal and financial feasibility of such CoHousing Projects for older people. This was due to report in early 2002. A consequence of this study is likely to be support from the London Housing Corporation for a Social Housing Grant input to the OWCH scheme - a support which may unlock public money for other CoHousing groups in Britain who wish to establish mixed tenure communities.

Since the OWCH group started, two broad directions have been followed: one, a process of community and capacity building by the group and two, a parallel process of research and outreach carried out by others. Taking the latter process first, the group won the generous support early on of the Joseph Rowntree Foundation which from 1999 funded me as a part-time consultant to the group. I assisted in their community development and acted as an intermediary with external agencies as well as a promoter of the CoHousing model for older people generally. Housing for Women, a small RSL in London, became the group's development partner in June 1999. It has been searching for a site and is likely to remain the landlord for the social rented properties in the scheme.

Community and capacity building is an essential prerequisite of CoHousing. Thus, by far the most important dimension of the OWCH project has been the steady growth and development of the group itself. Meeting regularly each month and also organizing a number of residential weekends, the group has grown in solidarity and purpose. This process has also generated strong informal social and support links within the group which are operative now while they are still scattered around London. Running its own affairs through a small coordinating sub-group and a number of task groups, the group has agreed policies and procedures for the future in a number of areas. Group members have undertaken training on issues such as equal opportunities and conflict resolution and, before taking up residence, will have been trained in housing management and finance. Skills in organizing, facilitating meetings, making public presentations and in computing have been enhanced and developed within the group. Persevering and maintaining unity and resolve in the face of a continuing wait for a site and support from a local authority has been difficult and frustrating. This is a problem facing intending CoHousing groups everywhere but it is a more pressing one for people in their seventies who feel that their remaining time may be limited.

Local authority support

By early 2002, the OWCH group were still waiting for a site to be identified in London for a block of around 24 flats to include owner-occupiers, shared owners and renters with shared facilities such as common room, guest quarters and a garden. London, where the group's members have their roots and social networks, is a difficult arena in which to develop and is subject to predatory developers, luxury developments and price inflation. Dependence on the help of one or more of the London boroughs in identifying and securing a likely site, possibly through a section 106 'planning gain' provision, has proved somewhat difficult. Family homelessness pressures, lack of land or the lack of a capacity for innovative and 'joined?up' thinking has meant that local authorities have not shown much interest in the hopes and dreams of this group of older women.

Once a site or building has been identified, other factors are likely to come into play which may point up a sharp contrast between Dutch and British housing policies. The price of inclusion in a section 106 requirement may mean no say on the design of their dwelling for OWCH members, who have their own enthusiastic design sub?group. It remains also to be seen whether the narrow space constrictions laid down for social housing for older people will afford them anything like the spacious, airy, light?filled dwellings they have seen in the Netherlands.

More crucially, a hurdle yet to be confronted is the convention by which local authorities in this country nominate 50% to 75% of the tenancies of social housing from their housing register. It is to be hoped that, like its Dutch counterparts, a local authority will view the successful achievement of a workable community of older people based on shared interests and activities and mutual support, as also a brave investment in their freedom of choice and autonomy. Diversity and choice for older people is the expressed aim of government policy (DETR/DH 2001). For the OWCH group to succeed in differentiating itself from any other randomly accessed housing development for older people, it must be allowed to choose new members for the social housing units on the basis of their support for the aims of the group and their age in terms of the age structure of the group. (CoHousing works for older people because it maintains a broad age range and therefore, hopefully, a high energy quotient and a low concentration of dependency.) Allocations on the basis of a narrow definition of housing need and a points system come nowhere near recognizing the essential ingredients for a sense of community. Already diverse in terms of social background, education, income, disability, nationality and sexual orientation, the OWCH group currently has no members from the black and minority ethnic communities, where the proportion of people who are older is of course comparatively small. The group is keen to reach out to older women from these communities in positive ways but there is no guarantee that women will wish to join them. It is to be hoped that the equal opportunities preoccupations of London boroughs will prove reconcilable with the efforts of the group to diversify and choose its own members. This remains to be tested. An external body's nomination of strangers to a housing development ? which is the prevailing norm in sheltered and other forms of social housing ? is not conducive to the formation of an active, living, sharing and supportive community as described above.

Central to this paper has been the awareness that Britain needs to address the challenge of ageing and also to develop a new mindset in terms of housing policy and practice in the light of high rates of single occupancy living. There is, as this chapter has demonstrated, a need for new thinking and positive forms of encouragement in design for greater flexibility, shared space for new social groupings, community formation and social connectedness. The stimulus offered by the CoHousing Community as a way of living ? a model which generates increasing interest among older people as more get to know about it and the OWCH project ? presents a challenge to policy makers and to the providers, builders and financiers of housing for the future.

References

Brenton, M. (1998) 'We're in charge. 'CoHousing Communities of older people in the Netherlands: lessons for Britain?. Bristol, Policy Press.

Brenton, M. (1999) Choice, autonomy and mutual support: older women's collaborative living arrangements. York: York Publishing Services/Joseph Rowntree Foundation.

Brenton, M. (2001) 'Older People's CoHousing Communities' in S.Peace & C.Holland (eds) Inclusive Housing for an Ageing Society'. Bristol, Policy Press.

DETR (April 2000) Quality and choice: a decent home for all.

DETR/DH (2001) Quality and choice for older people's housing: a strategic framework

Fromm, D. (1991) Collaborative Communities: CoHousing, Central Living and other forms of new housing with shared facilities. New York, Van Nostrand Reinhold.

Gann, D. (1999) Flexibility and choice in housing, Bristol, Policy Press.

McCamant, K & Durrett, C. (1994) CoHousing.. a contemporary approach to housing ourselves. Berkeley, California. Ten Speed Press.

VROM (1997) Huisvesting van ouderen op het breukvlak van twee eeuwen. Zoetermeer: Ministerie van Volkshuisvesting, Ruimtelijke Ordening en Milieubeheer

VROM (1998) Van Idealisme naar Realisme. Zoetertneer: Ministerie van Volkshuisvesting, Ruimtefijke Ordening en Milieubeheer.

Maria Brenton is a Visiting Research Fellow at the School for Policy Studies, University of Bristol. She has been funded by the Joseph Rowntree Foundation to assist the Older Women's CoHousing project, London

Strategies for creating CoHousing neighbourhoods

Previous chapters have described in some detail what can be expected from CoHousing neighbourhoods. It is less clear what the promoters of CoHousing initiatives could themselves expect in tangible support for their proposed neighbourhoods.

The modern world is full of a continually changing mass of formal and practical policies that will influence the shape of public and private services to meet social need. Central Government alone has a wide range of perspectives for shaping the intentions of new residential developments and the role of future housebuilding, notwithstanding the other views from local government, and from the private or voluntary sectors. Much space has been given over to public debate on ideas about creating 'sustainable' places to live, and the importance attached to this central concept will continue to shape much of the future. When current aspirations are viewed through the lens of CoHousing values, however, it could be argued that there is still a substantial gap between a policy framework setting the mould for new development and the practical frameworks for how real neighbourhoods are to be realised.

Local neighbourhoods can be just as important a place for where people live, work and meet, as the core urban areas and services that are increasingly put forward as essential to modern households. Clear examples of thriving and supportive neighbourhood environments can challenge a dismissive portrayal of 'residential neighbourhoods' as places of isolation or suburban loneliness. The supportive nature of CoHousing within neighbourhood developments needs to be promoted in a context of wider policies that can draw understanding of what strengthens neighbourhood identity within such new residential areas. The wider policy framework may then be used to shape how an insertion of opportunities for CoHousing and other community-centred development might emerge within the subsequent development.

The proper connection of the widest planning visions with the most intimate of community ambitions requires a breadth of policies and strategies to create real residential environments appropriate to those people who wish to live in them.

Bringing a shared identity to underpin 'sustainable' developments

While this is not the place to make a full comment upon all aspects of Government considerations about 'sustainability, it will be worthwhile to summarise briefly the recent format of key policies that are promoting the 'sustainability' of residential development. Such promotion has been a steady theme within wider policy development, although there has been no consistent manner or scale in which the central concept of sustainability (or indeed community) has been invoked. 'Sustainability' is put forward as much in terms of ecological issues, (and an eco-neighbourhood like the private-sector self-managed 'earth shelter' scheme at Hockerton fits such a renewable stereotype) as in terms of energy production, or 'mixed housing tenures or mixed-use and economic development' for the commercial life of city centres.

In recent years there has been a number of complementary approaches to policy development. There has been what can be termed a strand on the general values inherent in ideas of 'sustainability'. Drawing from the preceding exploration of Local Agenda 21 initiatives, the Government's National Sustainable Development Strategy, 'A Better Quality of Life', [DETR, (1999)] defined sustainable development - as an interdependence of economic, environmental and social well-being. It's focus should be to ensure 'a better quality of life for everyone, now and for generations to come'. Such values have clearly been instrumental in shaping the community plan framework instigated by the Local Government Act, 2000. This empowers local authorities to promote the social, economic and environmental well-being of their local population, and requires the production of formal Community Plans to be the guiding principles to shape cross-sector service developments and delivery.

Other policy change has followed an holistic approach to how structured development and re-development could relate to existing populations. The latest in a long line of area regeneration initiatives are the Single Regeneration Budget and New Deal for Communities programmes that have encouraged more integrated use of resources within 'deprived' neighbourhoods. The recent Neighbourhood Renewal Action Plan[SEU, (2001)] is both an extension of this approach towards bringing 'sustainability' into 'disadvantaged' communities, and an extensive agenda to reorganise mainstream service opportunities within such neighbourhoods.

There has furthermore been increasing attention to the likely character of new areas, especially in terms of what new housing development should be able to support. Consultative documents like Planning for the Communities of the Future[DETR, (1997)] have encouraged development bodies to adopt people-centred strategies within local initiatives. It set a clear marker for the Urban Task Force's Towards an Urban Renaissance report (1999) which highlighted different European examples of innovative developments. The subsequent Quality and Choice - a decent home for all(DETR, 2000), and the Urban White Paper Our Towns and Cities (DETR, 2000) and Rural White Paper, have all continued to focus upon how to strengthen people's commitment to the areas in which they live and work.

The concept of 'community' used within these various policy initiatives has included many different settings and scales for the number of households that could be involved. The examples detailed within the DETR report on Millennium Villages and 'Sustainable Communities' [DETR, (2000c)] associate 'sustainability with groups of hundreds of households, although Brown et al (1999, p.50)] had already identified "a major gap in our knowledge relating to sustainable housing indictors". The rhetoric of the current Sustainable Communities Plan(OPDM, 2003) is, however, just as explicit in conceiving that the 'sustainable communities' being promoted can stretch to thousands of properties at a time. It can be wondered to what extent this will address concerns raised by commentators like Grayson (2000), who reviewed contemporary perspectives of how the housing world might address this thrust towards sustainable urban communities. He summarised the factors likely to shape future neighbourhood development as : conservation of resources; choice of location and tenure; socio-economic change; and balancing affordability with cost. Chanon (2000, p.202) went further in noting that while the 'consent' of a neighbourhood's inhabitants may be required in order that regeneration or job creation schemes can function, lasting support to disadvantaged communities will require a proper awareness of what is "knitting communities together, furnishings friendships, invigorating local democracy and creating social cohesion".

Lately, Lock (in Neal et al, 2003) has usefully summarised the enduring and sustainable quality of new development as a 'collective task' requiring the blending together of a range of appropriate changes acting at the 'regional' scale, at a 'neighbourhood' level, and on a 'block' by 'block' basis. Real 'quality' development will come through a combination of planned activity acting eventually at all three levels, although it must overcome a real 'resistance to change' within strategic planning debates if it is to assist development to happen upon more open and intelligent lines.

He considers (op cit p.63) that the overall character of this 'collective task' should be discernible in how new development demonstrates :
- participation in the way it is planned and implemented
- subsidy from the value of the formal planning approval
- an expression of its locality in structure
- inclusion in who it accommodates
- a mixture of use and character
- a focus upon non-car mode of travel
- a well-connected public realm
- links to excellent public transport
- management in perpetuity by its citizens.

It is enlightening to realise how much of this up-to-date assessment of crucial factors has been anticipated by the principles of CoHousing development. All the core values of design, scale, mix and control are echoed in Lock's summary. And they are clearly able to point to an ongoing vibrancy that has created and sustained real successful neighbourhood communities, showing impressive levels of local collaboration and common life. Barton (2000) has misunderstood the complexity of this neighbourhood-form when he summarised it merely as a closely-knit route to share ecological management. He does provide, however, a useful description of 'cellular' neighbourhoods that will interlink a range of local services and residential catchment areas. This cellular theme echoes the application of 'intentional neighbourhood' principles within Continental examples of suburban developments, as in the Greater Copenhagen area and in Freiburg. Here 'intentional' principles have shaped the development of different clusters of 'shared' neighbourhoods within larger urban and suburban development. What has emerged is a patchwork of different discrete neighbourhood settings, with different degrees of shared spaces and facilities, each in accord with the preferences expressed by the groups of households residing in that part of the neighbourhood.

The conclusions of the recent Barker Review(2003) into the level and quality of current housebuilding in the UK have highlighted the meagre rates of new building taking place. Within its report are various references that only are the number of properties insufficient to meet modern needs, but also that the limited range of housing being built is insufficient to meet all aspirations. The appeal of CoHousing to place with such analysis will be the degree to which it can assist new development to be influenced by the intentions of would-be residents and demonstrate how neighbourhoods will be not just places to live or work but also to share. In this respect, the value of models of intentional neighbourhoods will be how they can provide a clear route to the satisfaction of community aspirations at Lock's 'block' or sub-neighbourhood level.

Strategic principles to promote new communities

Although central Government has acknowledged a prevalent tension between the promotion of 'sustainability' objectives and the 'maintenance of conventional policy perspectives' (DETR, 2000), it will be invaluable to identify principles that can prioritise CoHousing and other intentional neighbourhoods against the economic, social and environmental consequences of conventional policies. The development of a greater appreciation of the links between such consequences can then facilitate integration of these sustainable ideals into wider strategic and policy agendas.

What follows below are suggestions for amendments to different kinds of UK strategies and policies that could promote the qualities of 'intentional' neighbourhoods into established planning and decision-making frameworks. The suggestions have been made in terms of influencing principles of community well-being, housing policies, and design and planning codes to promote greater interest in a shared identity within local developments. The overall intention is to promote a strategic policy infrastructure that can encourage broad opportunities for the establishment of such local ideals. This should then at least permit practical opportunities to come forward that policies can require or oblige to support such community intentions in practice.

In the following points there is a constant interchange of the words 'collective', 'shared' and 'intentional'. At all times these terms have at their core the depiction of a neighbourhood development shaped through a complexity of interpersonal 'mutual aid' and collaboration. Modern ideas to living a shared' neighbourhood life by choice have not been the subject of much recent public debate. Academics exchange views on what could contribute to 'sustainable' communities, however invariably media attention on any group issues is either a piece on the needs of disadvantaged communities, or an article about a collection of households 'doing a commune thing' - invariably seen as a leftover from the 1960s and '70s. Policy development needs to be much more substantial in ambition.

1. Principles to promote new neighbourhoods with a 'shared identity'

• Include an understanding of the opportunities and benefits of intentional neighbourhoods within Quality of Life standards that are put forward as research indicators (see DETR, 2000b) for assessments of sustainable development.

• Apply CoHousing's understanding of community dynamics at neighbourhood and sub-neighbourhood levels within casework studies of recent appropriate residential initiatives, such as promoted under contemporary urban village and Planning though Design initiatives.

• Promote at policy-making levels from the Regional Assembly downwards, the potential for the ambitions of future residents to inform the planning and design of a range of different kinds of neighbourhoods within different large masterplanning developments. Invite ideas to come forward from competitions held to gather proposals for sustainable neighbourhoods.

• Assess the practical steps that local strategic partnerships responsible for wider neighbourhood design and development. Encourage community involvement to develop group ownership of neighbourhoods, and support community-controlled bodies - like social company structures, co-operatives, community trusts, and pending commonhold agreements - for example within new editions of Community Plans.

• Adopt explicit principles of an intentionality to new neighbourhoods within descriptions of the desired quality to what 'sustainability' should represent within local development - such as sub-neighbourhood targets for mixed-tenure and community-controlled development. Use these within local justifications for accepting or refusing formal proposals for new housebuilding : Lancaster's recent use of this principle to steer developments already over its Development Plan targets is a move in the right direction.

2. Principles for 'planning' policies

•   Regional Planning Guidance will increasingly shape the priorities of the statutory development frameworks at Local Authority level. A clear indication that 'intentional neighbourhoods' should feature within the range of developments promoted by regional guidance will encourage subsequent Local Planning Frameworks (the formal frameworks that indicate acceptable land uses and local priorities) to invite local schemes to include principles in support of 'intentional neighbourhoods'. The Frameworks could both invite 'collective' proposals from would-be residents or bodies seeking that end, and give specific encouragement to proposals that would demonstrate a clear connection to the final communities that will reside in the development. Maybe there could be a usefulness for a new class of land used for residential purposes - namely for 'collective residential use' - to facilitate granting formal approvals to proposals for explicitly holistic initiatives where this involves pairing private residences with locally-focused shared community facilities.

•   The encouragement of such principles could also be spelt out in key statements within additional 'planning guidance' issued by local authorities - such as currently undertaken in Area Planning or Design Briefs, Supplementary Development Guidance, or briefs for Priority Development Areas. This could encourage a combination of planning and design values to maximise opportunities for promoting site-specific ideas for 'shared' neighbourhoods within wider proposals. This could also be the means for encouraging targets for a 'high density' to new planning development to be focused upon achieving this in a variety of low and high rise solutions.

•   There will be a clear potential for the encouragement of a range of neighbourhoods within some urban regeneration schemes, plans for urban villages or urban extensions, or plans for entire new settlements. Larger developments are in any case likely to have to respond to standard planning requirements that they make provision for affordable housing within the total accommodation being proposed and provide for other community benefits. An encouragement for proposals to include elements of intentional' neighbourhoods will offer opportunities to combine market and affordable development within innovative mixed-tenure ambitions. The new-build CoHousing scheme in Stroud demonstrates just such a readiness to use private sector resources to subsidise the inclusion of other lower cost units.

● Local Authority guidelines that will spell out the terms and focus of formal planning conditions (whether these materialise in the form of current Section 106 planning agreements or in some other form, like tariff arrangements) could frame criteria for what intentional character should be incorporated within the overall proposed development.

● Planning strategies that seek to maximise the prudent use of environmental or energy resources will be able to exploit interest in renewal resources at the local and sub-neighbourhood level by promoting a joint 'stewardship' within shared neighbourhoods. The BedZed development is one approach that has capitalised upon such a planning commitment, however the guiding principles will be as applicable to schemes at more intimate scales.

● Given the increasing concern about the current low levels of housebuilding in the UK, there are proposals for a tax on land that has been bought for future development, but has remained unused for an unacceptable length of time. If such ideas are to be considered in more detail, it could be an opportunity to propose an obligation that at least part of a site be offered to a community-led initiative (at a reasonable price!) so that unmet local aspirations are offered a means of undertaking real development. And if there is case to be made for such obligations, then possibly there is a case to re-examine ideas for some nationalisation of land, in order that local priorities can be addressed in full.

3. Principles for housing policies

• Support for principles of intentional or other resident-designed neighbourhoods could be included within the housing strategies of the new Regional Housing Boards, and associated statements of intent from Regional Development Agencies and Regional Assemblies. This would give a clear signal to the community-at-large that needs for new housing are being viewed in the widest context.

• Amendments could be required, however, to change the cost indicators of regulatory bodies like the Housing Corporation's (which regulates use of grant subsidy for 'affordable housing') in order that a full inclusion of shared neighbourhood facilities is not compromised by inflexible restrictions to contributory finance.

• The strategic role that local authorities should adopt as promoters of inclusive local housing strategies could neatly encourage housing development bodies to support intentional neighbourhoods. Ideas for collective housing schemes could easily feature within the promotion of a range of residential solutions to satisfy wider policy aims & local aspirations.

• Estimating local interest in collective housing provision or intentional neighbourhoods should be woven into local authorities formal assessments of housing needs and demand. If the existing framework used to consider such needs is expanded beyond 'housing' needs to consider the wider context of 'community needs', local desires for a more collaborative neighbourhood life could receive higher attention. This could be combined with an active willingness at local authority level to bring people interested in 'collective' ideas into contact with another, as well as support other networking to this end. [It would be interesting if such an estimation of community needs could also influence the calculation of the various finances awarded to local authorities for service and developmental priorities.]

• Similarly, interest in the possibility of intentional or other shared neighbourhood settings could be sought at the time when households seeking accommodation register their needs to a local authority. A positive support for this could become an acceptance of local lettings policies that could respond to households expressing interest in accommodation of a collective or intentional character.

- As a further means of encouraging strong links between housing tenure and neighbourhood identity, neighbourhood residency could be promoted that is based on different forms of an area-based leasehold ownership (such as the pending commonhold tenure). This would allow residents to combine a marketable interest in individual property with a collective responsibility for an area, by virtue of collectively being the 'freeholders' - the body that ultimately issues the residential lease. Where some neighbourhoods so wish, a collective ownership could be strengthened through limits put upon any individual's right to buy their property's freehold outright. (This would reduce the possibility that future selling and buying of neighbourhood accommodation might allow people to buy into an area without them having a real commitment to its 'shared'/collective character.) A collective agreement (e.g. in the form of a clause in a lease) could also limit future sale prices in order to maintain a level of affordability to the next parties interested in buying into the neighbourhood's intentional character.

- Where there are plans to include something like an Investment Trust in local housing provision (as suggested by the Barker Review), its initial parameters to shape local investment could be required to provide a practical support for a range of local provisions, including that of community-controlled areas at sub-neighbourhood level.

- While it is unlikely that designs for intentional neighbourhoods will be the basis of Local Authority investment in existing housing stock, a redesigning of existing areas to incorporate ideas for more communal or shared facilities would be a clear means of demonstrating support for some 'tenant and resident participation' initiatives.

4. Design principles and design codes

• Attention should be given to the design of housing areas that will allow a balance between personal privacy and a common, shared identity. This should be geared towards a careful mix of 'private' accommodation, supplemented by 'shared' spaces and other facilities, all located within a neighbourhood that will provide other facilities for the use of its residents together.

• The physical layout of neighbourhoods should make deliberate use of architectural and design features to maximise opportunities for intentional and incidental social contact and strengthen local connections within the neighbourhood. The actual percentage requirements of open space in relation to the built environment should be flexible, so long as strong opinions from aspiring residents can inform the final designs on how that could be used.

• Design demands that focus upon high density development should promote different kinds of high densities - not simply the piling of more and more properties on top of one another. CoHousing-style development is well-suited to a low-rise but high-density provision, both in newbuild settings and in rehabilitated buildings.

• The key principles of Home Zones to minimise the imprint of traffic on or through neighbourhood areas, should be applied to desires for car-free and pedestrianised residential environments. An acceptance of lower parking requirements from the overall built development ought to be a minimum here and should provide another benefit of a reduced expenditure on road and hard-surface infrastructure.

• The design and location of a common building as a key site for specific local communal activity should be promoted. As a minimum it should be designed to include sufficient space for all residents of the neighbourhood to be able to meet together. Other ambitions to include practical management of ecological concerns - such as space for recycling, or a common energy supply system - would be relatively straightforward to incorporate into space given over to common or shared facilities.

• While a regular and personal contact between a neighbourhood's residents can itself ease local anxiety about crime or other anti-social activity (and by definition identify 'strangers'), it would also be feasible for IT services to connect neighbourhood properties together within a linked area-surveillance or home security system.

It might be fanciful to believe that the subsequent promotion of intentional neighbourhoods within the key policies noted above would automatically present CoHousing Groups with a myriad of practical opportunities for new site development. More likely will be the need of local Groups to themselves be active in 'selling' such principles to key policy-making partnerships at a local level. This would at least prepare the ground for a later approach to landowners, housing developers, social housing bodies, even the Development Control sections of local authorities (i.e. the planners who report on formal planning approvals), to see how CoHousing ambitions might fit with other proposals for wider residential development. That is, to see if they can offer a solution to how any wider proposals may be required to satisfy formal policy or planning obligations.

It could be wondered whether an interest in shared neighbourhoods might only be displayed by a minority of households. The Institute of Public Policy Research's report (IPPR, 2000) on housing preferences, and the DETR's official statistics on current housebuilding rates and property tenure [cf. DETR website], both confirm a continual rise in the numbers of 'private' sector homeowners to other sectors or tenures. The appeal of private home-ownership as the preferred choice of tenure would seem to be a given, so how might this square with proposals that promote collective neighbourhoods? Would the nature of the latter in some way automatically invite concern from homeowners about a detrimental effect on property investment values, because of some abstract prioritisation of 'community' values? Evidence from recent UK examples of where leases have been sold within intentional community neighbourhoods if anything suggests the contrary. The market value of the saleable interest within 'intentional neighbourhoods' appears to have appreciated considerably, and reflects a growing belief in the stability and marketability of similar neighbourhoods in Scandinavia and the US.

One could, of course, add a degree of scepticism about this supposed British obsession with 'home-ownership'. Is such tenure able to demonstrate, by itself, an automatic increase in social cohesion or 'well-being'? Surely other aspects of people's living standards will also be important to them? 'Home-ownership' may be the tenure preferred by many because they associate a financial investment with an increase in overall security. A different sort of 'investment' is a personal contribution to a collective endeavour, where that collective endeavour will also represent a very tangible sense of security, especially where it is irrespective of an individual's ability to provide much by the way of personal finances. Such a collective endeavour could still include opportunities for 'ownership', even opportunities for individual investment in properties. It is just that, in the context of jointly owning and managing an entire neighbourhood area and its facilities, this generates mutual consideration of seeing what is one's own interests as also one's neighbours' interests. And this can generate a strength and security beyond simple isolated ownership of property.

It is not difficult to point to examples of where national policy has in effect hoped that new groupings of households will spontaneously create a mutual and sustainable 'community spirit', but where this has not been materialise within real neighbourhoods in practice. It could be quite different if households were encouraged to be intimately involved together at the birth of ideas for new neighbourhoods, and thereby be ready to invest their time and energy into creating a supportive and shared neighbourhood environment in which they intend to live.

The number of ideas for new settlements or urban extensions do offer clear opportunities for an encouragement of new neighbourhoods to include those with the intimately-scaled 'intentional' ambitions as outlined above. While they might be thought to offer a challenge to some of the practices promoted by cutting-edge ideas for Millennium Communities or Urban Villages, they in fact complement such developments in their ability to assist in the delivery of real community-focused neighbourhoods at street level. Policies to promote such neighbourhoods offer an additional facet to new visions for urban and suburban development in how ideas for intentional neighbourhood communities' can be included within mainstream initiatives for new settlements. And they need not involve great difficulty or cost - it will be extremely straight-forward to weave many of them into a coherent policy infra-structure that can harness the modern enabling functions of statutory authorities to emulate the boast of contemporary American developments - *"creating communities, one neigh-bourhood at a time."*

PART TWO
Towards a Guide for CoHousing Development

A 'CoHousing Handbook' was produced a while ago for groups in the United States [Hanson, (1996)] and McCammant & Durrett's original book has something of a 'handbook' flavour in its detail on how CoHousing projects develop. Other 'guides' for UK neighbourhoods provide insight and advice into establishing 'sustainable communities' or communal living projects, [cf. Diggers & Dreamers, or the recent Practical Guide from the eco-community at Hockerton]. Nothing to date, however, has been produced that is suitable for the particular dimensions of CoHousing within UK settings, nor anything that brings together relevant legal, financial and design aspects within an advice-based framework. This is intended to be the beginnings of a UK Handbook for CoHousing Development.

Notwithstanding the comments made earlier on the core characteristics of CoHousing neighbourhoods, there is no one set of right principles for how a CoHousing project should proceed. Neither, unfortunately, is there any single way that a Group should behave that will guarantee its success. There is, however, a fair degree of experience that can be learnt from a range of other community neighbourhood projects. New projects are always likely to take on the particular characteristic of their locality and of the people involved, but that need not involve Groups avoiding what other projects already know to be productive. New CoHousing groups do not need to invent all their working environment from new, time and time again.

Recognising obstacles to the creation of new neighbourhoods

It is tempting to think that the appeal of CoHousing will be sufficient for it only to be aired to a discerning audience ready to appreciate its combination of privacy and neighbourliness, for it to turn them into yet more converts to the modern communal cause. Indeed, if modern communes and other intentional communities provide the idyllic environment described by some contributors to the CoHousing Network website, who would not wish to live in such a neighbourhood? Who could not be drawn towards adopting such ambitions for themselves, and put their own resources towards that goal? And with the high profile attention being given to the Government's current Sustainable Communities imperative (ODPM, 2003), surely the time is right for such collaborative aspirations - the future can only be positive.......

The reality for Groups looking to progress such intentional communities seems significantly different. Proposals for new CoHousing schemes come and go as various Groups keenly anticipate the building of new neighbourhoods in which to set down real roots, but gradually wither away from the frustration of not making this happen. Is the basic concept at fault? Are such neighbourhoods just too awkward for people to create for themselves? Or is there something that that lies at the edge of Groups' abilities to address - some constraint to the communal aspiration that is more fundamental to how any new neighbourhood developments are nowadays created?

The few examples of CoHousing communities that do exist in the UK will be an encouragement for new CoHousing aspirations, however having an understanding of what obstacles might impede new Groups, or sap their momentum, can be as helpful to their appreciation of progress as them being aware of what can move their plans forward.

Below are highlighted fundamental factors that Groups should consider may challenge them in their desire to realize the collective ambition, namely:

(i) the manner in which housing and land resources are effectively controlled by mainstream agencies in the housing sector works against provision for communal lifestyles, particularly those considered to be unorthodox.

(ii) that ideas such as CoHousing often contrast adversely with established ideas about sustainability or communal aspirations - the latest Government promotion of sustainable communities has little mention of intentionality as an acknowledged motivation behind community developments;

(iii) that the wider business and policy environment within which much modern housing development must take place will require Groups to develop suitable business and political skills in order to maintain a complicated project, and accept compromise if the ideal solution is not forthcoming.

Understanding mainstream housebuilding resources

The options open to Groups that wish to establish new 'ommunities are intirnately entwined with securing the necessary resources to make any UK residential development a success - namely land, buildings, finances, and people. Of these it is particularly the first three that are bound up with the manner in which housing has become multi-faceted activity with its own professional disciplines and interest groups, regulated by statutory institutions, and influenced or squeezed in various ways by modern market forces. What we innocently label as housing is actually a pseudonym for a complicated industry of complex bureaucracies and financial features that now determine the design, development and provision of virtually all new accommodation in the UK. Groups seeking a collective solution to shared housing and neighbourhood aspirations need to appreciate how and where this institutionalized framework so affects the regulation and use of key housebuilding resources.

There is an intricate policy background in the UK, increasingly dictated by central government, that prescribes the numbers of new dwellings it is believed will be necessary to house the nation's population over a coming period. Increasingly, formal requirements are being set by Government policies and agencies for the amount of new accommodation to be created within each region and sub-region of the UK. These formal requirements then become the key context for regional bodies to prepare Regional Plans (and sub-regional Plans) to secure the allocation of sufficient land for housing development. These requirements are then repeated as requirements at a local level within the over-arching Local Plan land-use frameworks prepared by local Councils (i.e. City Councils, District Councils, Metropolitan Authorities). Other formal governmental codes of guidance'-furthermore demand that the range of dwellings to be provided should offer a suitable range of provision that will be appropriate to meet a range of local needs, as identified via appropriate local research and formal assessments of the widest housing need and demand. This complex prescriptive approach is then the basis used to confirm what sorts of housing development will be appropriate for different urban & rural areas - particularly for what size of settlements, or designs for house sizes, mixture of tenures and households.

The actual permissions for new housebuilding remain in the hands of local authorities in their role as local planning authorities, although there has been a dramatic shift in their activity of the previous century. Local authorities are no longer significant housebuilders in their own right, but have been reduced to being part of the mechanism that regulates or encourages how other bodies provide the new properties required to satisfy national policies and meet local needs. Most local authorities have little finance available to use for new building - the vast majority of housebuilding is in the domain of the private sector, with a clear emphasis on producing units for sale. The prevailing values of contemporary UK society that private ownership of individual property units is something to which all households should aspire has increasingly enabled the housebuilding sector to focus upon the production of that type of commodity above all others. Private sector housebuilders routinely complain that their own developments and profit will be particularly effected by any formal obligations to provide properties for other tenures, particularly rent. A consequence of this response is the extent to which the small public subsidy still available for housebuilding has been directed by the housebuilding sector towards low-cost ownership schemes. As recent research has shown [JRF, 2002], planning approvals granted for new house-building have simply not achieved the range of 'affordable' housing sought by current Government land-use policies, nor the intended level of provision without public subsidy. It will be interesting to see if the current proposed changes to key policies like Planning Policy Guidance Note 3 : Housing [HMSO, 2003] will change this situation.

It would, however be naive to assume that what remains of state subsidy towards housebuilding will be that much more sympathetic to aspirations for communal endeavours than the private sector. Public subsidy towards new or established housing provision involves close adherence to the prevailing policies and guidelines applied to the social housing sector by a major body like the Housing Corporation (and followed by local Housing Associations). Such policies are instrumental in setting the overall tone for determining what local housing needs are accepted as outstanding (i.e. unmet at present), and what should be the use of public resources in the future. Prescriptive guidelines are set for the use of funds for different sorts and sizes of accommodation. There is a strong emphasis on ideas of appropriateness and for what sort of provision is considered appropriate for different sizes of households in the context of the housing that available for allocation to people 'in need'. It is extremely difficult for a single-person household to obtain any self-contained dwelling provided through public or quasi-public subsidy that is bigger than a 'single-bedroom' sized dwelling (by definition, a flat), even though records of household demographics clearly point to the limited appeal or flexibility of such units.

The Government's latest Sustainable Communities policy is but the newest initiative in a long line of policies focused upon the geographical and regional dimensions of national demands for new properties. This 'industry' has furthermore become dominated by a focus upon the production of the number of units to satisfy a projected need for new properties. Significant parts of the national economy are now geared around the production and the consumption of such units, and one constantly hears debate about the costs of producing units in ways that could still achieve high returns on the investment required.

The ODPM's recent Sustainable Communities Plan[HMSO, 2003] seeks to bring regional housing and spatial land-use strategies closer together (plus other reform to parts of the national planning framework from the recent Planning Green Paper [HMSO, 2002] - like changing Local Plans to Planning Frameworks). Regional planning policies will then be geared to fit closely with regional housing strategies produced by new Regional Housing Boards and both used to shape the distribution of state funds for housing services, and the allocation of areas for new development.

Two key features of this focus upon the production of individual housing units are important for group-based proposals or aspirations like CoHousing.
(a) It has made other residential scenarios, such as communal scenarios, seem increasingly out-of-the-ordinary & unnatural.
(b) The prevailing conditions of a market economy geared to the supply and consumption of pre-formed housing solutions offers declining opportunities for people to shape or control their own provision.
The result is that 'housing' is now both an activity carried out by, and a commodity provided by, a wide range of public and private sector bodies on behalf of others. It has become almost entirely removed from notions of people providing for themselves. (It might be argued that the position of self build housing has a strong quality of self-provision, although generally it is more self-management than self-build, and it is almost exclusively for individual households and one-off units).

Yet while such public bodies have a major control over the policies for the use of such public finance or the allocation of land within formal spatial planning frameworks, there is actually little public opportunity to steer, amend or change those policies. In theory there are opportunities at prescribed times for local people to make comments on the Local Plans of local authorities, or to comment each year on the Housing Corporation's investment strategies. In practice, however, comment is returned almost exclusively through the established channels of organisations connecting with other organisations, used to the process of steering their responses through well-established systems within and between trade and professional bodies. And the established organisations are certainly aware that loud rejection of government intentions could result in subtle reduction of the opportunities to secure grant finance for further development - which for most housing bodies that operate in the subsidised housing sector could be a disastrous outcome.

In practice therefore, there is little public ownership of any vision behind the policies for public funds or the designation of land resources, nor of the targets or intentions to which such resources will be applied. Neither is there much genuine public ownership of any visions for how new residential areas could or should be created, nor the values that new housing developments could reflect, nor for what support could be directed to the establishment of a range of local communities. Even where there have been innovative developments over the years of a more collective neighbourhood nature - such as for new housing co-operatives or selfbuild organisations - the prevailing statutory frameworks have sucked the innovation back into bureaucratic procedures through which subsequent applicants should be required to proceed. It has been a similar experience with the recent report on the potential use of Social Housing Grant to support the Older Womens CoHousing Group in London, [H4W, 2002]. While it can be useful to see the subject within a national research framework, the report has nevertheless ended up with a strong bias towards the needs of Housing Associations rather than seizing the opportunity to craft an innovative means of supporting new practical approaches to neighbourhood development.

Yet if intentional community groups are to make an appeal for some element of state-funded subsidy or support for their plans, it is precisely to this conservative and highly-regulated system they will need to approach. Some members will have to be low-income earners or in insecure housing to allow a group the chance to put forward a request for such support, and they will inevitably be forced to argue that their plans should be prioritised above some other proposals for the use of local resources. Groups will be required to understand the motivation and mind-set of housing bureaucrats whose usual concern for who is or is not 'in need' will not automatically mean they are used to debating the use of developmental finance directly with such individuals 'in need'. Yet a Catch-22 in so promoting a communal solution to meeting 'housing need' is that this will inevitably involve arguing that a solution is unlikely to appear immediately : by definition this can mean that one cannot be sufficiently 'in need', (or else one would not be able to wait!). The project's appeal for some public resources is likely to fail if evaluated against other demands that may appear more urgent.

Ideas for group living schemes are also routinely on the receiving end of enormous skepticism. The response from professionals in the housing sector s commonly that "people do not really want to be part of groups" and are not likely to be very successful at it, because modern social engagement has placed privacy and separateness above other interactions. Ideas for group schemes are almost expected to fragment and fall apart - regardless of whether or not the holders of such views have sought the real level of local interest in 'group' or 'communal' ideas from local people. Usually the formal plans and policies are not even obliged to investigate that interest. The extent of cynicism that groups can encounter also extends to accusations of self-interest and bias - they can be accused of competing for scarce local resources (such as public subsidy or a prized site) that are more necessary for the needs of others. The role of the professional regulators of the use of state resources has in fact become one of being gatekeepers of access to those resources. It is standard to hear within professional discussions the anxiety that the arbitrators of public resources should not encourage ideas for future developments when they cannot see how those ideas can be satisfied - the stock approach is that this 'should not raise expectations'. It is no surprise that the consequence of this is actually to depress general expectations that local housing and community provision could ever be that different from the established orthodoxy of the present.

Understanding ideas on community sustainability

It is something of a paradox that although there continues to be development of national policy to focus national planning and housing guidance towards the establishment of 'sustainable communities', it is not easy to determine what constitutes a 'community' - let alone a sustainable one. Consultative documents from central government like Planning for the Communities of the Future [HMSO, 1997] may have highlighted ideas for people-centred strategies within local initiatives, however they have systematically failed to recognise the place of ideas on communities or neighbourhoods of an 'intentional' nature. Rather, many policy statements read as if 'new' communities will spontaneously come together and acquire a longevity and vibrancy of their own simply through the provision of decent housing, or regular transport, or a clean natural environment, or good schooling or local employment opportunities. The focus of a great deal of support for 'communities' is moreover not based upon the creation of new communities or neighbourhoods. It is deliberately addressed towards existing deprived areas, such as the population of poorer inner city areas, or bleak housing estates on the edge of large towns and cities. That is, towards helping existing communities that are believed to require assistance to knit more durably together - be this by the provision of more local services or other financial opportunities, and by seeking to invigorate local democracy. This is a key aspect of the ODPM's current policy focus [2003] upon creating a sustainable social cohesion within local communities - even though it is not that clear from the policy exactly what or how such 'cohesion' might be achieved, nor the basis on which 'communities' could be supported.

Concerns about sustainable development have predominately focused upon energy savings or upon protecting the natural environment, however Fairlie (1996) has already documented how local authorities have been loathe to supported some proposals for low-income/low-impact schemes. This has not been a simple refusal to accept the ecological principles at stake. Other innovative 'ecological' schemes in the private sector have been successfully piloted over recent years - the interest in the ecohomes at Hockerton and in the recent BedZed development in Greater London demonstrates a developing interest and market for similar schemes. Rather it points towards how local planners are instrumental in the classification of innovative communal approaches to local community life, and can display a readiness to dismiss new ideas as 'unsuitable' even where projects have been able to demonstrate plenty of public or local support for collective aspirations.

What seems missing from this development of sustainability policy is a readiness to accept the dynamics of emerging communities at a neighbourhood level - e.g. within new residential development - as a aspect of a total understanding of local sustainability that is worthwhile to consider. Ideas for what constitutes a community's 'sustainability' rarely devote much attention to the interpersonal dynamics between a neighbourhood's residents, or their collective self-determination over a local environment. Conclusions about the sustainable setting of a community usually focus instead on the natural environmental issues, or upon energy uses. Metcalf (1998) is in a minority of commentators who have considered the sustainability of intentional communities coming together on a day-to-day basis (including CoHousing settings). He accepts the environmental and economic dimensions to 'sustainability', however he notes that there is an equally important dimension of social and cultural sustainability. By this he refers to "the human community demonstrating it can endure as an amicable social unit" - in particular at a scale of social contact that is meaningfully important to local people. Ironically, Metcalf has some fears for how much a CoHousing neighbourhood may cater for individual households to the extent that it will not match the savings of energy and resource he believes is more achievable from single unit groups, like communes. Indeed he asks whether the sole interest of CoHousing groups is really for *"a pleasant way to live, pretending they are part of a sustainable communities movement, while ...... clinging to individuality ensures that nothing is achieved"*.

The character of this wider 'amicable social unit' is still struggling to be understood. Policy proposals for the desirability of 'mixed housing tenures' or for 'high density' development fail to highlight the absurdity of applying the same term 'community' to denote a variety of different things. It is used as much for a single street or group of households, as for discussing some thousands of households in new urban suburbs or town 'extensions'. Yet this overlooks the real importance of how the scale of built development will influence upon how households actually relate to one another in a meaningful manner - how they might develop the character of an 'amicable social unit' that is a key element of aspirations in people who deliberately wish to create neighbourhood communities. The larger the extent of any residential development, so the greater the opportunity for there to be a dominant anonymity between the people resident in the area. It will include those who relish such anonymity as well as those trying to forge new identities in or from their new surroundings. The scale of new residential developments is therefore a crucial aspect in the opportunities for community-minded aspirations to gel together, and can be as much an obstruction to the development of vibrant and connected communities, as the presence of an alienating design in itself. To the common one-dimensional view of community ought to be added an understanding of the scale of sustainability at the level of actual neighbourhoods, one that is based upon a practical understanding of how communities & community members can be enhanced through a deliberately intimate, interpersonal scale of development. This reflects the attention to scale given by successful intentional communities, where deliberate designs and characteristics encourage a very close involvement of the households inside each locality and with local recreational facilities and community-based spaces they create and manage for themselves.

Developing the skills of CoHousing Groups

As if the above monopolisation of resources (and ideas) by established institutions is not enough in itself, groups looking to create new communal neighbourhoods in the UK need to assess how they might interact with such agencies. The background to most community involvement in Britain is an increasing lack in general society of any real awareness or skills for what is required for collective action on community development. Participation in public life seems to be on a continual decrease, even where that participation has been reduced to placing a vote in municipal or national elections. There is substantial lack of awareness of political decision-making structures at all levels - local, regional and national. This is compounded by a lack of experience in taking part in groups or partnerships that might wish to challenge the impact of those structures upon local life. Part of the appeal of CoHousing is precisely that it addresses a keenness to join in local activity with one's neighbours, although political action is not an obligation for living in a CoHousing community!

In order to gain the most out of what abilities and skills a group may already possess, they will need to adopt a 'business-minded' approach to their community goal. Tasks that will help the group progress their community project need to be clearly defined, along with recognising the value of adopting and implementing trusted techniques that can help in carrying them out. Groups do need to take a stance on 'pragmatism', especially when dealing with the real decisions required to move their project forward. Too many UK projects use up significant energies on rudimentary debates, such as on the kind of legal identity they should adopt, or in which geographical direction they should seek a site to acquire. It is easy to allow an overall momentum to stall for lack of any agreement on the parameters of key decision-making. An 'ideal' site might be desired by all, but if that is not likely to materialise it is important to reach early agreement on what would or would not be acceptable in its place. Paradoxically, while the level of community activists in the UK may not be huge, there is plenty of community-based experience and knowledge of skills that new groups can tap into. New groups with no history of collaboration do not have to feel that they must approach their problems as if no one has ever solved them before. They can draw from what has gone before them, and use inspiration from a range of recent and distant advisors [cf. Eno & Treanor (1982)].

Groups need to challenge their own attitudes about their relative expertise and inexpertise, and be ready to challenge members on their commitment to the group's stated intentions. Achieving and maintaining a credible momentum is all-important, both to sustain the commitment and belief of would-be members and for any formal or professional partners with whom a group may liaise. Community groups obviously need to challenge such professional pessimism with a clear promotion of the kinds of community successes that do exist, and the sound reasons for such success. If a group's endeavours appear to be fading away it will be likely to lose existing members, and unlikely to attract new ones. The maintenance of such credibility does, however, itself represent a demand on a group to take itself seriously and to have the clear-sighted attitudes to promote its plan and its project in a thorough and efficient manner. This may come through finding professional support and engaging the formal services of suitable agents used to working in property development. Care must still be taken, however, that such contractual partnerships do not turn out to be dominated by the 'expertise' of the professionals or professional bodies engaged - especially where their actual experience is limited of CoHousing ideas or the unorthodox! Groups will need to recognise the dangers of neglecting to properly manage what will be become in effect their own appointed 'project managers'. They must therefore be assiduous in developing the skills and the attitude to do this increasingly confidently and effectively. It will be not be helpful for groups to simply assume that any formal 'partners' will do the best for them out of a sense of altruism, a surprising common assumption from people unused to managing the work of others working for them.

For the majority of groups that have managed to get their collective heads around such internal organisational issues, there remains perhaps the biggest decision of all -

namely what kind of development will turn out to be economically possible, and what range of issues will such a decision set into motion? Will a group's resources be sufficient to create the kind of community it wants? And will those be sufficient to compete for the acquisition of a site on which to build, or be able to attract loan or entrepreneurial finance, if this is required?

For groups without sufficient private assets, the intention to seek some state subsidy towards part of their scheme's development will set demands in motion of a different sort of competition. A number of current UK groups are in this last position, seeking to combine private resources with an appeal for some state funds, in order to develop cross-tenure communities with a mixture of properties for ownership and for rent that could house those member-households who have already come forward. Such a collective endeavour could still include opportunities for 'ownership', even opportunities for individual investment in properties. It is just that this would then be in the context of jointly owning and managing an entire neighbourhood area and its facilities, rather than being solely a focus upon the ownership interests of individual households. There would be the added context of this being a challenge to adapt to the interests of the whole communal neighbourhood, and reject any previous assumptions that even in a mixed community the needs of a certain tenure should outweigh an equal consideration being given to the needs of all.

Considerations

POINT ONE

The mentality of the housing and planning professions' status quo interferes with the possibilities for community-minded-groups to develop their ideas in that established procedures for identifying housing and community 'needs' are focused upon house production in terms of what individuals need - individual housing solutions for individual households. Even if those households occupy property in a new development alongside other households, the prevailing approach is to plan and provide for the accommodation of so many separate and distinct households. The consequence of this established view on how to plan for new housing and neighbourhood development is that ideas for significantly different neighbourhood development are seen as worryingly unorthodox. Examples of inspiring and sound blueprints of community developments, like CoHousing, do need to be broadcast to challenge the naivete of the orthodox view and to promote the profile of 'intentional communities' in general. There are, moreover, many contemporary interests concerning social policy with which such promotion could now be associated. Successful neighbourhood communities can demonstrate that they offer social stability and a sense of local permanence. Mutual support between households, a mix of households of more than one tenure and a support for a vibrant approach to the subject of a 'neighbourhood' managing local services are a clear example of how to harness the social capital that a range of key policies are seeking to strengthen.

POINT TWO

Supporters of intentional community aspirations need to exploit existing formal policy-making mechanisms in order to insert a support for collective principles that could generate opportunities for championing local interests, if and when those interests emerge. Ideas and support for new communities could feature within planning, design, and housing frameworks in order to raise the profile of how such communal projects might establish themselves and compete for resources or support. The insertion of such values into a range of national and local policies would encourage a greater identification of such interests. There is much that a sympathetic policy infrastructure could do to encourage groups to believe there could be genuine support with which to shape future neighbourhood developments.

POINT THREE

There is significant potential for a range of different kinds of neighbourhoods to be included within the large 'masterplanning' designs for new urban and suburban residential developments being developed in many parts of the UK. Intentionally-minded Groups need to bring their ideas about intentional and shared neighbourhoods into the processes that will evolve proposals for the separation of larger urban/suburban development areas. into a patchwork of discrete neighbourhood settings. It ought to be possible that such processes can evolve a range of different shared spaces and facilities some of which are shaped by the preferences of self-identified groups of households. The Government's national policy development on requiring a percentage of affordable dwellings to be created within new housing areas should be seized as a lever by groups keen on acquiring land for a new intentional community. Groups could offer themselves as an existent source of interest in such property (i.e. as customers!), providing they would have the opportunity to help shape it into a more collective nature. This could go a long way to allaying the anxieties of private developers that the application of this policy in practice will only result in having to house households who will have no real interest or commitment in the long-term well-being of that new neighbourhood.

POINT FOUR
The core CoHousing principle that communities take the key decisions about membership and property transfers may also take some time to be acceptable to the wider property development 'industry', who have a powerful influence over national legal and housing practice. It will be beholden upon aspiring 'intentional community' groups to review the skills they require to adopt a more business-like approach to achieving their endeavours, and be firm in their search for the most suitable partners to help them achieve their goals. This may require a degree of compromise that was previously held to be unpalatable, however this need not be a one-way issue. 'Intentional community' groups have a great deal to offer modern urban and planning policies - particularly the prospect of a very real shortcut to the creation of the 'sustainable' community those very policies hope will emerge from new residential developments. For that reason alone, such groups ought to take seriously the prospect of having a role in delivering part of the neighbourhoods of the future.

Legal Structures for CoHousing Bodies

It is a recurrent concern to new CoHousing groups that they should give careful consideration to having a formal legal status, in particular a formal identity that will be most suitable for the kind of community they are planning to create. What established communities have already used in the past is of interest here, albeit that members of some new initiatives might feel they need to be convinced that previous developments will still be relevant to their own situation. More than just a dry consideration of abstract constitutions and legal formats, there is a keen awareness that the options and choices of different kinds of legal status can be fundamental to the shaping of a whole community.

Groups come to the subject of legal identities with a series of key questions in mind, principally about how the law can frame the community 'ethos' that lies behind their common aspiration. While various general commentaries can be found on UK legal structures [cf. Contacts / Bibliography] it is not a straightforward matter to glean from them what will be most useful for a community of private households having a shared, semi-public dimension. And if the private facilities to be encapsulated in dwellings for individual households are to be based upon one or more kinds of property tenure, then is there some particular legal framework that will turn out to be most suitable for this particular aspiration? Could different kinds of property tenure or ownership by the CoHousing households, or indeed a mixture of different tenures in one neighbourhood, predispose a project towards one legal identity rather than another?

Questions and concerns about the range of potential CoHousing scenarios would include at least the following:

1. Is there any one legal structure that offers the best assistance to a body that is acquiring a site or building for a CoHousing project ?

2. Is there a legal structure that is best for a CoHousing body seeking to develop communal facilities and accommodation for ownership, or one that is better for a mixture of ownership and rental tenures , or one with some other combination of tenure ?

3. What type of legal structure might best suit a body of members collectively owning the freehold of a CoHousing site, but selling or issuing leases on individual units of accommodation to its members (and the terms of the sale spell out rights and obligations about the communal neighbourhood) ?

4. Is there a legal structure that best suits a body that may not own the freehold of a CoHousing site, but where members would wish to have safeguard rights and obligations to the property and facilities contained on the site?

5. Is there a legal framework that will be a suitable structure for a CoHousing project based solely on outright ownership, where individual households own the individual freehold of their property ?

6. What is there in any legal structure that would best detail the CoHousing body's formal obligations to its CoHousing community?

7. Is there a particular structure that provides the best framework to separate the individual CoHousing members' responsibilities for their own accommodation and responsibilities to the community as a whole?

8. Is there any legal structure that will best preserve the communal identity and character of a CoHousing community, regardless of changes in the individual households living in the accommodation?

What follows below is not a detailed answer to each of these points (this would risk being too presumptive about what Groups come to decide) but a summary of UK legal structures usable for 'community housing' projects, and comment to separate their individual characteristics.

Basic Issues : Legal identities

The legal identities or types of formal incorporation that a CoHousing Group might consider will basically include:

(a)   registration as a Limited Company
(b)   registration as a Co-operative
(c)   becoming a registered Charity
(d)   creating a Trust (ie: a Land Trust or Development Trust)
(e)   establishing a Partnership
(f)   registration as a new Commonhold Association
(g)   registration as a Housing Association

The accompanying comment will detail their differing usefulness to CoHousing projects, and then focus comment upon the likely usefulness of a couple of these formats.

(a) Registration as a Limited Company
Formal registration as a Limited Company is via an established and (usually) straightforward process to register the process company's Memorandum of Association with Companies House in Cardiff. Occasionally Companies House will challenge the wording of part of a proposed constitution for the new body and stipulate the need for revision or amendment. Two types of company exist under UK law.

a) The first structure - a Company limited by share - is based on the organisation being controlled by share-owning Directors who will have a collective and shared liability for all the action and effects of the company. The worth of their shares can accrue a monetary value, and shareholders may have the opportunity to amass unequal proportions of the limited number of formal shares that has been issued. The absolute liability of Directors in such companies is unlimited, in as much as each Director may become individually be liable for the responsibilities of the whole Company (and other Directors acting on behalf of the Company).

b) The second structure - a Company limited by guarantee - is one where the organisation has been established for a wider community benefit instead of for the monetary benefit of its Directors. In such bodies each Director will have a limited liability (usually to the value of one share fixed at £1) because it has been accepted that the outcome of the Company's action is ultimately to create a benefit for others besides just the body of Directors. The Directors will remain collectively responsible for the formal effects of the company.

Usefulness of company format

All the CoHousing schemes that have been successfully developed in the past few years have taken one or other 'company' approach. Thundercliffe Grange in Yorkshire set up a company limited by share to organise the equitable financing of the project from members' private resources and the granting of leases on individual properties. The original Frankleigh House project set up a company limited by share to provide loans for members, while the Community Project in Sussex and the Stroud project in Gloucestershire have both been formed around companies limited by guarantee.

Some CoHousing groups have considered whether companies limited-by-share could be suitable for permitting different levels of share-based investment (and decision-making) by a project's founding members. While this is technically feasible, it has been contrasted with the ability of a company limited-by- guarantee to maintain the egalitarian basis between members that is usually considered essential to CoHousing communities.

(b) Registration as a formal Co-operative

These are based upon formal registration as a form of Industrial & Provident Society(I&PS) through the Registrar of Friendly Societies in London. [The RFS is now become a part of the FSA Financial Services Agency.]

An I&PS society is a long-established framework for organisations set up for the support and benefit of its members, and can be traced back to at least the establishment of original co-operative societies in Victorian England. Various kinds or classes of I&PS societies now exist, and there are recognised sets of Rules for the establishment of different kinds of such societies - known as Model Rules - that other organisations may use to register as that kind of body. Each set of Model Rules will lay down the minimum number of original subscribers required to support the formal application of registration.

One of these classes is for registration as a formal co-operative body, and has been over the years as a framework used by a host of housing or worker co-operatives. [Confusing, another class has been for a 'Co-owning' society - however this is not the same as a co-operative and is not as flexible a set of Rules.]

Usefulness of co-operative format

A set of Model Rules has now been registered by Catalyst Collective (a body supporting housing co-operatives) and is intended to be a set that may be used for new CoHousing initiatives. For groups keen to adopt a recognisably egalitarian identity, an I&PS structure is a tested framework that has persevered through the years. This new set of Rules is intended to clarify the role of a single body promoting a unified benefit for a membership combining members in rental properties and members in some form of home ownership.

(c) Becoming a registered Charity

Formal registration as a new body with Charitable status is via acceptance of a suitable constitution by the Charity Commission. There is not a standard format of a charity body as such, although there is plenty of advice available from the Charity Commission on the types of activities that may be accepted as suitably 'charitable' to gain a body that formal status. it is possible for a completely new organisation to apply for immediate registration of 'charity' status, although it is not an automatic process, and it can take significant time and effort. Nowadays the seeking of such status tends to be more something that existing bodies pursue, through a submission that existing aims, objectives and activities could be accepted as 'charitable'. The Charity Commission is increasingly wishing to explore whether or not existing charitable bodies can perform the activities for which a brand new body is being proposed, rather than grant the status to yet more bodies.

Usefulness of charity format

It might be thought that the collective and supportive nature of CoHousing development would lend itself to charitable objectives and be suitable for acquiring a charitable identity. This seems unlikely to be the case. Notwithstanding the quite technical methods of how the Charity Commission reviews what will be suitable for 'charitable' purposes, charities basically exist as a framework for the efforts of some people to be working for the benefit of others. Importantly the Directors of a charitable body are not allowed to acquire any material or financial benefit from the operations or assets of their charity. That alone is likely to exclude the would-be residents of a CoHousing project from being able to act within a formal charity structure set up to provide for their neighbourhood or take part in its decision-making. A charity could own a neighbourhood or property, but it would have to be answerable to others than to the CoHousing residents. This may prove too difficult to respond to the fairly personal character of a CoHousing community's day-to-day operations.

The above points would not prevent a CoHousing body from establishing a registered charity as an educational body, i.e. to promote the ethos or principles of CoHousing as a general activity, focused upon people who could be informed about CoHousing. It would, however, still need to be careful of any material support it could seek to give to an established CoHousing community if the residents of that CoHousing body and the Directors of the charitable body turned out to be more or less the same people.

(d) Establishing a Trust

Establishing a trust under UK law is a further example of a body with charitable purposes, even if the receiver of that charity is a single person, (such as setting up a trust fund that will pay a child an income on them reaching a certain age). Similar to the reference to a body having 'charitable' aims and objectives in (c) above, a trust could be created to hold land and property providing the operation of such holdings is acceptable under the formal purposes for which the Trust has been created. Modern applications of the Trust format are that of structures designed to promote economic or local employment opportunities for under-resourced communities, such as a Community Development Trust which has become popular as a legal structure for community-led business and property developments. Typically, Development Trusts are legal structures acting as a legal partnership between local bodies and interests from the private, public and voluntary sectors, with a clear remit to steer the activity and benefits of the body towards the interests and well-being of a defined local community.

A further innovation on the principles behind community development trust are proposals to create a new legal framework for a Community Land Trust, along the lines of similar bodies already operating in the United States. A Community Land Trust (CLT) [cf. CCH Feasibility Study, 2002] is a "community-owned body that holds and uses assets on behalf of the community it serves [....] the CLT model is based on it being a non-profit-distributing body owned by its members, where the ownership of the freehold (or long leasehold) of property assets is transferred to the CLT, or the CLT takes a legal charge over the assets. [....] the CLT will then use this asset base to raise finance to invest in, or provide additional assets or services for community benefit ..... especially in order to find solutions to complex problems of poor housing and disadvantaged neighbourhoods." The intention behind this model is not simply to be a pragmatic device - to be successful a CLT will have to make sense and provide the tangible benefits to potential investors, otherwise they will not invest their assets or their energies in it.

Usefulness of a trust format

Whilst having a Charitable status can increase the opportunity of a trust organisation to raise funds, (there are a number of grant-making bodies that will now only direct grants or other finance to registered charities) the acceptable activities will be restricted towards the proper beneficiaries of the charity. Notwithstanding some potential advantages of such charitable status, bodies like development Trusts or CLTs will principally be organisations that work for the benefit of the wider, public community, rather than a well-defined set of households within a CoHousing neighbourhood. The Development Trust or Community Land Trust models do not exclude the possibility of financial benefits accruing to individuals, such as in terms of support for employment enterprises in which individuals have a stake. A body that is necessarily controlled by a combination of wide community interests is, however, not be a body that will be exclusively responsive to the more inward-looking and private aspects of CoHousing neighbourhoods where the CoHousing households wish to have direct control over collectively-owned assets. The nature of 'Development Trust' frameworks would be unacceptably limiting in relation to CoHousing projects, if the framework involved a formal decision-making role for people who could not themselves live inside the scheme.

Interestingly there has been an increasing movement by some housing bodies originally set up with a trust identity towards them changing their formal status to that of registered companies or registered Housing Associations. It is increasingly recognised that a trust format can introduce unhelpful limits where there are modern responsibilities from housing and property development that are not in themselves intrinsically charitable activities.

(e) Establishing a formal Partnership

There exists in UK law the means for a group of individuals to sign themselves up to a collective or shared activity, without formal incorporation as one of the bodies listed above. It is based upon forming a partnership that will be the basis of taking defined responsibilities for a prescribed set of subsequent actions and agreeing a specified sharing of the outcome(s), including any liabilities. It would also usually spell out the position of each party in the partnership if, at the time a liability is required to be met, it is not forthcoming under the terms of an original agreement.

Usefulness of partnership format

While such legal agreements are the basis for a number of formal 'partnerships' relating to property development, they tend to be between bodies that are well versed in such legal mechanics and in the arrangements and responsibilities that follow from them. For a completely new CoHousing group this may be too insecure a situation to be the sole framework between members with which they would undertake complex project development. Not having a recognisably formal structure whereby the detail of members' responsibilities, obligations, and ultimate liabilities are spelt out could also be an impediment to securing the necessary confidence of potential partners. Where a partnership format might become relevant is when a legally established CoHousing body may enter into a partnership with another body - such as a housing developer. This could then detail the arrangement for how a developer will provide accommodation and facilities to the CoHousing group and the terms under which the Group will acquire them.

(f) Registration as a Commonhold Association

The formal registration of new Commonhold bodies is proposed to be via a standardised process managed through Companies House in Cardiff. Commonhold tenure is a new form of ownership as an alternative to leasehold ownership, and eventually is expected to be its replacement. The Commonhold and Leasehold Reform Act 2002 received Royal Assent on 1st May 2002. [Not all of the Act's new provisions have come into formal effect, but will commence incrementally over a coming period]. The new system of Commonhold will be introduced as matter of choice for developers building new flats, but there will also be means for conversion from existing 'leasehold to a Commonhold basis.

In a Commonhold' the owners of flats (the unit-owners) will own their properties in perpetuity (equivalent to freehold) and their title-deed will also give them common membership of the Commonhold Association, which will own the land, the structure of the building and the common parts. All unit-owners will have a vote in the operation of the Commonhold Association and thereby have some responsibility for the management, maintenance, repair and servicing of any buildings. There will be no separate landlord; the unit-owners will share ownership and management of an entire site or building through the Commonhold Association.

The practical management and governance of the building will

be according to the Community Statement, agreed and produced by the Commonhold Association. This, in effect, will
replace a lease in setting the conditions of occupancy and will
be a public document, registered at the Land Registry.

Usefulness of Commonhold format

It is not yet known if this tenure that is designed in the main
for lease-owners to have a new right to a collective ownership of a property's freehold will be suitable for a situation
where the residents of properties are a combination of owners and renters together. Leaseholders in the Commonhold
scenario are envisaged or described as the purchasers of leases, rather than as the widest kind of lessee described in UK
law. This could be either an owner-occupier or a rent-payer,
for in law both are holders of a lease, that describe the terms
on which they occupy their property. Given that the whole
'Commonhold' status is being introduced slowly it will be
interesting to see what it might offer to CoHousing aspirations. At present it is too early to state how useful this change
will prove to be.

(g) Registration as a Housing Association

The concept and description of a Housing Association is
sometimes mistaken for or confused with that of a Housing
Co-operative. This is a significant mistake as there are radically different aspects to these two types of bodies and radically different premises for and from which each has been established. A Housing Co-operative can be summarised as a housing body controlled by and for its own members - in the context of the formal Model Rules already noted in (b) above. A
Housing Association can be summarized as a body controlled
by a formal Board of Directors that provides housing and
related services to others - namely to the residents households in its property. These households cannot include the
Board of Directors. The legal structures of Housing
Associations include a number of the legal identities noted
above, (in the main bodies now have a company and a charitable element to their overall incorporation), however all have
additionally satisfied the criteria required for formal registra-

tion, principally under the terms of recent Housing Acts. The term is now quite precise and not open to any body to use. [N.B. The housing legislation also refers to 'Registered Social Landlords', (RSLs). This is a term that defines Housing associations in terms of being registered and providing a landlord service to the tenants of low-cost or subsidised housing, but also applies to some other bodies that could qualify for that description under the terms of the Acts. For purposes here, an 'RSL' will be held as being synonymous with 'Housing Associations'.]

Usefulness of Housing Association format

In theory the legislation that governs how bodies could acquire the status of housing association could be open to new community-housing bodies. In practice the Housing Corporation (with whom registrations are made) is no longer keen to register completely new organisations if they have no previous track record or experience of being a provider of housing services for 'social benefit'. The process of regulation by the Housing Corporation has also become an enormously protracted and bureaucratic business, covering all aspects of an Association's being and services - governance, property management, property development, relationship with tenants, relationship with the public, etc. It should be considered unlikely that the Corporation would grant this status to a new CoHousing body. 'Housing Associations', as the main type of body that could still receive public funds for new housing development, are more likely to be organisations with whom a CoHousing project might do business, rather than a status it should aspire to secure.

Considerations on Legal Identities

POINT ONE

It is understandable that CoHousing Groups feel anxious over which kind of legal identity may be the most suitable for their project. It can therefore be a practical benefit for Groups to consider the formal constitution and framework of a Company Limited by Guarantee as a kind of benchmark against which other legal frameworks could be evaluated.

By weighing up the powers, responsibilities and structures of a body registered as a Company Limited by Guarantee each Group could evaluate if this structure will be sufficient to provide the reliability and formality that its members wish for their neighbourhood project. Certainly, if this formal structure cannot satisfy a Group's aspirations in abstract - for example, where members may wish to have a share structure that can accrue in value - then an alternative registration will need to be explored. Rather than remain almost paralysed in uncertainty about what different incorporation might offer, Groups could proceed in the knowledge that if they cannot better the Company Limited by Guarantee, that should be sufficient at least to go forward from here. What Groups need to be wary of is becoming fixed in a constant state of uncertainty and thereby never moving forward. Where uncertainty persists about long-term legal structures, some Groups will find it useful to register as a formal body like a Limited Company in the short-term. This will provide an immediate benefit of a formal legal identity through which partners or future members could approach the project, whilst also providing time to agree what long-term legal identity the group might adopt.

POINT TWO.
Groups should remember that an initial formal registration as one kind of organisation, like a Company Limited by Guarantee, does not preclude them undertaking other registration(s) in the future. For example, members of a Company Limited by Guarantee could still register as a Co-operative body at some future date. Having one legal identity does not preclude the same people also registering as a second or different organisation, and holding two identities at the same time. Groups may believe that a Company structure is most suitable for the physical development part of their project, but that a Co-operative structure will most desirable when properties are in place and day-to-day management tasks come to the fore. A formal arrangement can then be set up that establishes appropriate connections between a Group's two legal identities, and details the respective responsibilities and obligations of the two legal bodies. A Group could also plan to

use one structure for certain roles, then when those roles are finished, create a second body to carry other roles forward and close the first organisation down. What is important is that initial decisions need not be forever binding over a Group, and there will still be other opportunities to consider alternative futures in the fullness of time.

POINT THREE

Whatever kind of organisational structure appeals to a CoHousing Group, it is wise to consider this from the perspective of other bodies with which one may have to work. This will particularly be the case in planning to embark upon one or other form of 'partnership'. Most other organisations will be familiar with the identity of Limited Companies. Not all will be familiar in working with Co-operatives. A potential partner's sense of unease about a CoHousing body's identity could undermine their ultimate support for the CoHousing project. If that seems at all likely then Groups should be able to consider a pragmatic approach to initial identities, in order to help their project progress.

POINT FOUR

Research into the legal formats and tenures that might assist a mixed-tenure CoHousing project using Housing Association development finance, was funded by the Housing Corporation during 2001-2. This has tentatively come to the conclusion that a CoHousing body could register as a Company Limited by Guarantee or as a form of housing co-operative.

POINT FIVE

Two full examples of formal constitutions are provided in Part Three that are suitable for registration as either a CoHousing Company, Limited by Guarantee or a CoHousing Co-operative. Both these two types of legal structure are ones of which many bodies and agencies in the housing development world will be familiar. For CoHousing Groups looking at 'mixed-tenure' projects and thereby likely to think about securing public funds such as the development grant available to some Housing Associations, these structures will represent a known framework within which formal roles, responsibilities and liabilities are all distinguishable.

The essential characteristics of CoHousing neighbourhoods have already been explored in different chapters above. The work of McCamant & Durrett (1988, 1994) has been fundamental to identifying these characteristics as:

(a) Designing for intentional neighbourhoods
(b) Private and common facilities
(c) The right scale for community dynamics
(d) Resident control and management

The first three are immediately identifiable with the design and physical dimensions of a CoHousing neighbourhood, whilst the ability of a CoHousing group to be in final control of key design decisions is crucial to ensuring that the overall detail of the proposed neighbourhood will support the community's core ambitions. Design issues therefore do lie at the very heart of what will assist aspirations for a new neighbourhood to be realize a truly CoHousing character.

The final design and facilities of a CoHousing neighbourhood are what will distinguish it from other approaches to 'people-oriented' designs. For example, 'CoHousing' has an approach on keeping traffic to the edge of a neighbourhood that is quite distinct from what can be acceptable to the contemporary philosophy of Home Zones (to say nothing of the intention to share neighbourhood life, that has no equivalent in the basic Home Zone approach).

To maintain the clarity of what distinguishes CoHousing design from contemporary UK principles of residential and neighbourhood design, the following table sets out the key contrasting elements:

Features of CoHousing Design	Features of Contemporary UK Neighbourhood Design
Neighbourhood architecture is intended to maximise intentional & incidental social contact, to bring neighbours into visual & verbal contact together.	There is a clear focus upon maximize household privacy to the exclusion of other contact. There could be some 'surveillance' over public or semi-public areas.
Neighbourhoods are predominately pedestrianised. The main open space is to encourage all households in the CoHousing neighbourhood to mix.	There is still a predominance of car use accessing all individual properties. Significant parts of housing areas are devoted to roads and hard-standing.
The size of a community is considered crucial. [between about 10 - 40 adults] It needs to be large enough for people to be absent without this being problematic, but not so large as to prevent people from establishing proper relationships with their neighbours.	There is no equivalent appreciation of size or scale that will stem from the wider built development on the relationships between neighbourhood residents. Policies to increase site densities are not accompanied by any understanding of how to achieve a high quality of social contact or sense of local identity.
Siting of internal spaces where people spend significant time (like kitchen areas) is deliberately towards outside communal spaces.	Prevalent UK housing designs accentuate the privacy of internal uses away from a contact with neighbours.
Private garden areas, where provided, are on a modest scale, after a priority is given to communal space(s).	Designs usually focus upon private entertainment and on wider public open space. There is much less consideration of communal space shared by households.
Design and location of a common building is considered fundamental for community identity. It should invite people to it, as they pass on their way to & from home, & be large enough for all residents to meet together at one time.	Common or shared facilities are not usually planned for local relationships but for much wider and impersonal areas. Local facilities are not seen to underpin the development of local identities or relationships in being a form of shared 'domestic space'.
Parking areas & play facilities are placed close to 'common' facilities to enhance community contact between all members.	Parking & play facilities are tucked away on sites where it is hoped they will not intrude into others relaxation. Facilities can be very one-dimensional & age group focused .

Springhill CoHousing Community Stroud

Basic Issues : Design principles

In reviewing how actual designs have materialized within real CoHousing communities, Zahle & Mortensen (1992) summarised how the above characteristics have brought about a number of different design categories :

Networks - where the housing and common buildings are randomly placed.

Halls - where the entrance and access to private accommodation is from a large hall used for communal activity.

Circles - where dwellings are grouped around centralised common facilities.

Streets - with housing placed on straight or angular lines, sometimes covered by glass.

Windbreaks - which group dwellings together around and towards the common facilities.

Multi-storey - where a multi-storey block has a range of private or communal facilities on different floors.

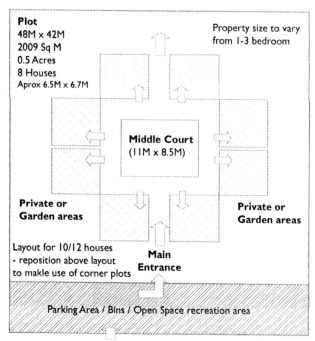

Main Entrance to Neighbourhood(inc;Vehicles)

Small neighbourhood on a half-acre site.

Design Considerations

POINT ONE

When considering ideas for a new neighbourhood, UK CoHousing groups may not find it that easy to visualise the amount of properties and facilities that might be built on a site under review. To assist in some of this deliberation an example of a small-scale CoHousing layout has been provided that suggests how to create a small neighbourhood of 8-12 properties, including common facilities, on a half-acre site. An actual site would not necessarily be the exact shape of this example, however it provides a suggestion of what on a modest proposal could achieve if that is all a group is able to consider. A variation of this layout could be extended for larger sites, and other facilities included if larger space allowed. In terms of overall density, this number of properties per half-acre represents a scale of land-use density of between 40-60 properties to the hectare - certainly above the current minimum levels being promoted by government policies.

POINT TWO
The layouts that have been used by UK CoHousing projects to date certainly cohere with the categories identified above. The hall variety has predominated, using buildings which had been previous large country house types, with internal separations for private domestic use and for shared community use (e.g. Thundercliffe Grange and Frankleigh House).

The Community Project's rehabilitation of the ex-hospital site in Sussex represents a form of a network layout, given that different sorts of buildings are to be found in different parts of their site. The actual siting of the main common house building is probably not where one would place it

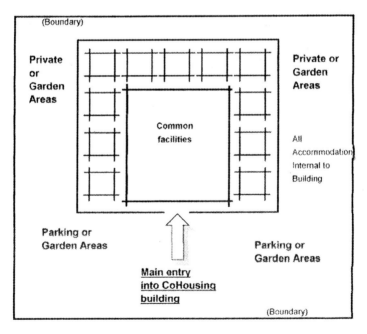

Hall Layout

if starting on completely blank ground, as residents can come and go to private dwellings from the road and the car park without needing to approach the common building. The amount of room within the common building is, however, of a variety and quality that many communities would be more than happy to have!

The new-build project at Stroud represents a combination of layout type. It clearly has some properties arranged alongside and opposite each other, as in the street category, but it also has the general layout of a circle in that the dwellings are curving towards the common building occupying a fairly central position, albeit on different levels of the site.

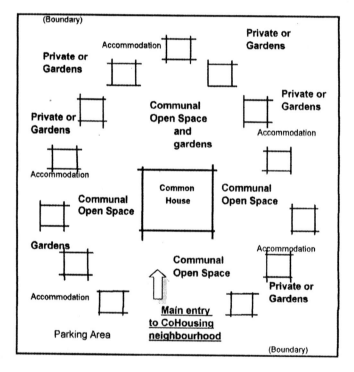

Circle Layout

Springhill CoHousing Community Stroud

POINT THREE

The design of CoHousing neighbourhoods will be centred upon opportunities to bring the community neighbourhood together within a range of daily and other ad hoc situations. Having a 'common house' that is at least big enough to bring together all the neighbourhood's residents at one social event should be seen as a minimum here. This is not the same philosophy as other 'lifestyle' schemes being promoted within the private sector, which seem to focus upon the recreational service or facilities that people could make use of. Such proposals for a laissez-faire leisure-based contact with the neighbourhood will be a quite different design than those neighbourhoods that explicitly support households into ever closer and more co-operative relationships together.

POINT FOUR

It is inevitable that new CoHousing projects will require detailed input from a designer or architect to put shape to how a particular site or property could be adapted to satisfy

CoHousing aspirations. What is not inevitable is that groups need to defer to the design expertise of others to the extent that they end up with design proposals that do not reflect their ambition because the agent has not kept close enough to meeting instructions.

CoHousing groups will need to work with an architect or designer who is appropriately experienced in working with collective community projects, and who is used to achieving positive solutions. That is to say, CoHousing Groups need to engage such professional skills as a formal 'client' in their own right. Depending on the nature of the particular project, this may require negotiation with key partners (such as a Housing Association) in order to establish a clear rela-

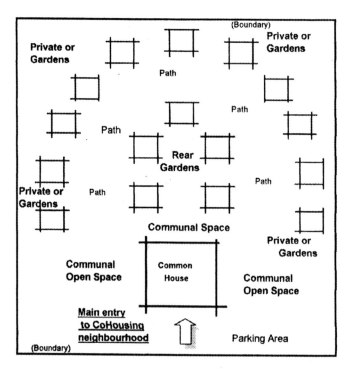

Windbreak Layout

Thinking About CoHousing

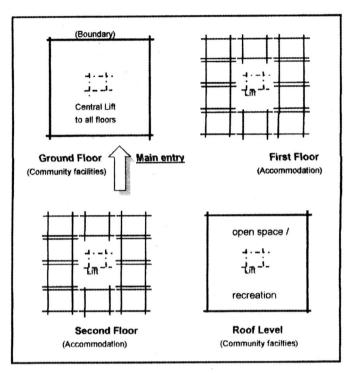

Multi-storey Layout

tionship between Group and the design agent and clear lines of accountability between them. It is crucial to establish that the design skills are being engaged for the ultimate benefit of the CoHousing community, and will be paid for by them both in cash and in living 'with' the result. This is too important to defer to other bodies, or to institutional procedures that are not used to accepting the abilities of neighbourhood groups to take on such responsible roles.

For some groups, finding a suitable design agent or architect may best be achieved through inviting bodies to return an 'expression of interest' that would be the first stage in being 'interviewed' for such an appointment. The next stage would then be a more formal interview, undertaken by the group, at which an agent's credential and experience could be examined in more detail.

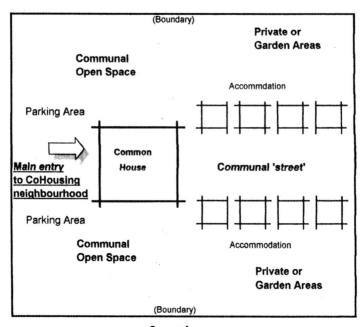

Street Layout

Springhill CoHousing Community Stroud

11 questions to ask a Designer / Architect (or other Agent) during interview

1. What is their understanding of the term CoHousing?

2. Have they any experience in visiting a CoHousing neighbourhood?
[and if yes, what detail can be given ....]

3. Any experience of working with or being part of a CoHousing project or Group?
[and if yes, what detail can be given ....]

4. What has been their experience of working with community groups?

5. Any experience of working with mixed-income initiatives?
[and if yes, what detail can be given ....]

6. How have they involved people from a group into working overall design ideas into final solutions?

7. Who from the agent's office has been involved in any relevant work, and what were the details of that work and role?

8. Who from the Agent's office would be involved , if appointed, and what has been their specific experience?

9. Will they be available for meetings at evenings or weekends, if required ?

10. Are they used to being just one agent in a wider project, where another agent may manage their input?
[If yes, what detail can be given ....]

11. What would be the basis of their fees?

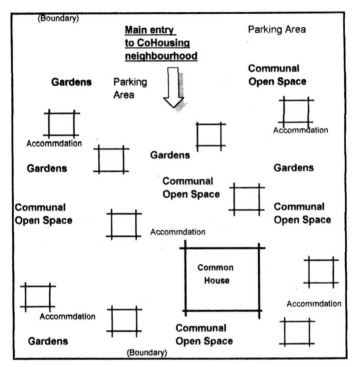

Network Layout

Part of such a formal process of appointment would be to set clear parameters of how the relationship is to be a business relationship. The ambition of creating new communities in the manner promoted by the CoHousing ideal can be a little intoxicating even for engaged professionals : a Group needs, however, to feel confident that key design decisions and evaluations will still be brought back to the collective body for consideration, and not taken by the professionals beginning to believe it is now 'their' project.

Funds and Finance Systems

After locating a suitable site on which to establish a CoHousing project, having the finance that will be suitable to turn the ideas into reality is probably the most crucial issue that will occupy a CoHousing group's attention. The crucial element here is that of finding suitable finance. It is one thing to plan for obtaining sufficient money to meet development expenses, yet quite another to consider the terms on which it may need to be repaid and any impact this could have on the dynamics of the CoHousing community. It will be of little purpose to develop a new community, but be so beholden to the conditions under which money was obtained that members will not be able to live in the property, or find that it could be at risk if sale to property investors as second homes.

The purpose of the comments here is to help Groups think realistically and plan strategically. CoHousing Groups will need to make realistic assessments of the actual options available for their project, and to which their actions may need to be addressed. In particular they will need to understand the extent to which their desired finance for CoHousing development will be to many other bodies just more finance for property development. Adopting a mindset that is able to structure a business strategy to address the issues important to property development will stand Groups in good stead.

The different stages of a property development project may not require all the required funds to be available at once - different amounts of funds will be needed to cover costs of site acquisition, development fees, and final construction. A CoHousing Group should plan for how it could have some finance available early in the life of its project, as it should not assume that even preliminary work (such as initial site investigations) can be done on the basis of any credit or deferred payment.

Basic Issues : finances

Groups may approach the task of securing funds for CoHousing in the UK with the hope that support will exist here in ways similar to other countries where it is well-established. At present this is not the case. In Scandinavian countries, after the first Danish schemes were privately-funded by their households, a range of subsequent developments have benefited from public funds, both for rent and for a mixture of rent and ownership options. Holland has been even more accepting of using public housing funds to develop CoHousing schemes, and has sustained an emphasis on schemes for older people, and on funding CoHousing support agencies. (Indeed, support for CoHousing schemes in Holland represents just one part of a collective approach to meeting housing needs for a significant percentage of the population). As an opposite to such use of the public purse, the enormous development of CoHousing schemes in the United States has been almost exclusively funded by resources from private households building schemes for outright ownership.

In comparison with such other countries, the current situation in the UK amounts to neither one thing nor the other. Although there are significant public monies still put towards general housing development, there is no automatic source of funds in the UK that will be available for 'CoHousing' development. The few CoHousing schemes that have emerged in recent years have basically relied upon resources from private sources - that is, from the kinds of finance that can be secured for general property development, and usually repaid by dwellings purchased by individual households, probably with mortgage finance. To consider what opportunities might be available to, or sought by, future schemes, particularly those seeking to establish mixed-tenure communities, it will be worthwhile to summarise the kind of basic financial resources that are relevant for housing development in the UK within the following categories:

a) Development loans
b) Private funds or private mortgages
c) Public sources
d) Other finance

Development loans

Traditionally, housing that is for sale for in the UK is generally built and sold by private housing developers, using either their own resources or private financial arrangements to cover their build and development costs. (The small exception to this is basically building carried out on a self-build basis by independent households). Invariably a development loan is sought from banks or major financial lenders. The overall economics of the project will then include calculations and assumptions of anticipated sales income to repay the loan (and interest), and provide a sufficient profit to the developer to plough back into further developments.

Private resources or mortgage finance

Some CoHousing development (like the Community Project) has been comprised solely or mainly of members who know that they can afford to purchase the created properties on the completion of the scheme. The combined resources available to group of households - based on savings, or the value of their existing property elsewhere, or their household's ability to repay mortgage finance - has then become the basis for planning the project's overall costs, and for what households could pay when development is complete. Notwithstanding that understanding for what happens at the end of the project, there will still be a need for a Group to have funds available as working capital to met costs incurred during the overall development period. This is more than likely to require formal loan finance that all members will commit themselves to providing and repaying during the time a scheme is progressed. Securing some monies from members at an early stage would be cheaper here than planning to borrow virtually all the funds from a third-party lender, as well as being a means of members demonstrating their commitment to, and faith in, the collective project.

Public sources

It is sometimes thought that as CoHousing is a robust example of a community-centred aspiration, it will be sufficiently impressive to guarantee material support towards a proposed CoHousing project from the local authority. Certainly local

Type and Explanation of Housing Tenures	Usual Resources Required
Freehold Ownership. Outright ownership for unlimited length of time. (Usually without any 'conditions' attached, though might be subject to a covenant about subsequent use or sale.)	Housing sold on 'ownership' tenures are traditionally built by private housing developers, using private resources or other standard financial arrangements. Some 'development loan' may be used and repaid through sales income.
Leasehold Ownership. Ownership of property for specified length of time. (Usually with 'conditions' attached, inc: formal terms of relations with property 'freeholder'.)	
Low Cost Homeownership. (LCHO)Property for outright or leasehold ownership marketed at reduced price, possibly with other conditions attached.	
Shared Ownership. Property sold on basis of part ownership and part rent in tandem with a body like a registered Housing Association, sharing costs of upkeep / repair. The purchase of 100% of the equity is usually possible - the tenure is likely to be a form of leasehold ownership up to that point.	Housing for tenures that with some reduced cost to the resident household are usually built with the assistance of public funds, such as grant finance made available to Housing Associations. The Association also usually requires other loan finance, as the grant available will not cover all a project's costs. Grant tends to be only repayable if there is a substantial change in property ownership, such as dwellings moving entirely into private ownership.
Affordable Rent. Property let by social housing bodies (like Housing Associations) on terms that are less expensive and usually more secure than rental accommodation in the private sector.	
Commonhold. A new 'collective' ownership of freehold to be available to a group of leasehold owners.	Likely to be similar arrangements as for existing ownership tenures.

authorities can be keen to see new community initiatives develop, however nowadays local councils rarely have the funds to give support towards all the initiatives they may wish to assist. Their resources are under intense pressure to be sold on terms that can realize the biggest possible income or capital receipt, in order that the authority can invest the finance in other services to meet community needs.

It used to be that local authorities were able and pre-pared to act as the providers of loans or mortgages for local housing provision, or as the guarantors of mortgages or loans gained elsewhere. While this is technically still permissible, (there still is a general 'power' of local authorities to use its resources towards 'community benefit') it should be consid-ered extremely unlikely that local authorities can nowadays provide significant material support for something that will appear to be just of benefit to a group of private households. Likewise with any idea about the role of local authorities to assist with house-building : while local house-building is still open to local authorities in theory, in practice the constraints put on their overall levels of public spending has meant that most Councils have ceased building houses directly. Instead finance to assist local housing development is channeled to local housing associations for such bodies to build in tune with local housing 'strategies' agreed by the authorities. Local authorities have, in effect, been left creating the objectives for local housing development and housing services that other providers should meet.

The public funds to assist such development come through the Housing Corporation, a quasi-governmental body with the role to support and regulate housing association activities to provide 'affordable housing'. The Corporation has a key role under the Government's recent Sustainable Communities Plan and its new Regional Housing Boards to oversee the allocation of housing development finance that is being targeted to meet the housing needs identified in new Regional Housing Strategies. (For CoHousing to draw from such finances, the ideas of intentional - or at least neigh-bourhood - communities will certainly need to feature more prominently than is the case at present).

A hope of some CoHousing groups is that their local authority could be prepared to offer resources like a site to 'community-focused' initiatives. In view of the constant pressure upon local authorities to maximise the financial return or 'best' receipt from the sale or disposal of their assets, there can be no automatic surety that a CoHousing scheme could receive some such subsidy or financial benefit. Some material support could also require conditions that a Group would need to consider most carefully (such as the terms on which it would have to accept the nominations of some households in need to live in the community's properties).

Other finance

(a) For the comments above about the likely constraints on public finance used to assist the development of 'affordable housing', similar reservations can be voiced about the likelihood of CoHousing being supportable from 'urban regeneration' initiatives or from EU funds. Such finance is usually directed towards building proposal that will seem to benefit large numbers of people, in particular in relation to assisting their prospects employment. While it is not impossible to present CoHousing as part of, or contributing to, wider benefits, public funds cannot be that reliable for the core development finance that CoHousing schemes will require.

(b) It might be thought that funds from Charitable sources should be available somewhere to assist low-income households or with small resources. Notwithstanding the comments already made on the restrictions of a body with 'charitable' status to provide benefit to its Directors, it is now extremely rare for the 'charitable' grant-making bodies to assist with any capital build costs of general housing projects. Such bodies are well aware of the funds distributed via the Housing Corporation and do not want to complicate the bigger picture of how 'subsidised' housing costs are met.

(c) Given the planning requirements on major housing projects to provide for a range of tenures, this could be one avenue for a CoHousing group to explore - namely that of reaching some 'partnership' agreement with a developer on how part of a larger site could be used for CoHousing development. Such an agreement may not even require much actual development finance up front, although a Group's members would presumably be required to commit themselves to taking the CoHousing properties on completion, and be clear on their separate obligations for acquiring their individual properties for rent, ownership, or whatever.

Finance and funding Considerations

POINT ONE

It will be important for groups to make a long-term assessment of all the development finance that will need to be repaid. It will not be realistic for a group to rely upon gifts, donations, legacies or other sums that might be 'given' to it - rather it should be assumed that all finance will require repayment and then consider what the that repayment is likely to require of its members. Groups should also be wary of any reliance upon finance that could undermine the ability of the CoHousing community to manage their future neighbourhood. The possibility of investment - for example from some funds via the public sector, or from an 'entreprenurial' property developer - could seem appealing, yet would be a problem if the terms of redemption was to suit the financier, rather than the CoHousing community. Groups need also to be careful about some members offering to invest more finance into a project than the worth of what one property would represent. If such a member needed to leave in the future (or perhaps died) how would the community redeem their investment if there was only one property to become vacant?

POINT TWO

A group's approach to raising funds collectively needs consideration of what form of legal identity may be most appropriate to different providers of finance. Groups will need to gauge which bodies are familiar and comfortable of working with formal co-operatives; some providers are more used to working with limited companies, and may feel uncomfortable with anything else.

POINT THREE

Groups should separate the collective tasks required for securing the finance to develop their project from what will be eventually required of people individually, such as their individual payments for the properties on completion. The total costs of a CoHousing project will include all the domestic housing plus all the communal facilities, including the 'common building'. It will be crucial for Groups to structure the apportionment of all these costs into the separate requirements funded by individual member-households in a manner in which providers of finance can feel comfortable. Describing the communal facilities as a separate building could appear to be an unnecessary expense to mortgage lenders, who are only used to funding individual self-contained properties. Describing the facilities as 'rights' to be enjoyed by property residents, spelt out for example in the form of a lease, is likely to be more understandable and thereby more supportable.

POINT FOUR

The green or ecological finance institutions - such as the Ecology Building Society or Triados - have specific spheres of interest, and are not automatically a source of development finance for a sustainable community. The Ecological Building Society has targeted lending towards building done by individual households - such as self-build projects. Triados have been more active in supporting group activities, and have listed basic advice about 'financial planning' for CoHousing projects on the CoHousing Groups website [see 'Contacts']. They had an involvement in assisting Frankleigh House and made funds available to the Community Project (though the finance was not subsequently needed). Their procedures can, however, demand lengthy liaison and discussion, and may not always fit with how project's take final shape.

POINT FIVE

A set of questions for groups to use when considering how to secure key support for their project is provided.(P200) They are set out as the basis of interviewing and appointing a Housing Association or a developer to be the group's main agent. Associations and housing developers are well-versed in arranging housing schemes and dealing with whatever permissions, planning approvals, grant confirmations, etc. as may be required by the nature of each project. It could be a substantial departure from their usual experience for such bodies to be engaged as an agent to a community group, however it will have an appeal to some! A group should think through what arrangements would allow their project to progress but where they still retain control of key decisions. If this can be achieved through appointing another body to be a scheme agent (and act as advocate on its behalf with formal bodies.) then groups should give this serious attention.

POINT SIX

Some groups may hope that a 'self build' route offers the opportunity to develop at lower cost than buildings developed by a paid construction contract. Notwithstanding that finding funds for a group self-build project is not itself straightforward, the demands and tensions of 'group self-build' projects are often under-appreciated. 'Self-build' work is an endeavour that requires significant inter-personal skills between a group's members, (like the skills required by a CoHousing project from a CoHousing group) on top of which an extensive commitment is required to carry out the demanding physical work. Both scenarios are a collective approach to life that is not nowadays a central part of many people's daily lives. This sets very real challenges to the people planning and undertaking such activity. Running the demands of self-build together with the demands of CoHousing is a truly ambitious plan! Realistically, CoHousing groups determined to pursue some element of self-build work will be wise not to plan beyond some building work of the common house, or individual households finishing off their internal décor and facilities to the serviced shells of dwellings (the option taken by the Community Project).

POINT SEVEN

A CoHousing group may need to be clear from the local Housing Benefit system what level of rental benefit would apply to members in rented CoHousing properties that do not have waged employment. The granting of such benefit is assessed in terms of what is locally considered a suitable degree of space and living standards for different sizes of household, and in some areas for different parts of the local authority district. The level of such benefit could be an important factor in overall calculations of members' available income on scheme completion.

POINT EIGHT

Some CoHousing groups also have ambitions for developing neighbourhood facilities like nursery or education facilities, or space for employment-based workshop space. It is not impossible that such facilities could be included within new development, however it is unlikely that much public finance would be available for such costs, certainly not if they are planned for just the CoHousing households and not for a wider number.

POINT NINE

The majority of existing CoHousing groups have the desire to develop 'mixed-tenure' schemes, combining properties for ownership with properties for rent on the same site. This will almost inevitably require a group to consider securing some kind of support from the public sector, and shape any Business Plan accordingly. Privately-financed schemes - i.e. one basically just for ownership properties - are likely to be more straightforward to organise. They can afford to focus upon households having access to a level of financial resources that should cover the project's build costs during its development, and buy the properties on completion.

POINT TEN

It might be thought that members of groups who could put their own resources (like mortgage finance) into a CoHousing project are in some way 'paying more' towards the project than members who reside in properties for rent or some other low-cost tenure. This will be an artificial distinction to make. A project's costs is likely to require bringing resources together from a number of sources, without all of which the total scheme could not proceed. Any view to emphasise ownership amongst some members would risk making a divisive distinction. A real neighbourhood will be 'owned' by all its residents, regardless of tenure.

The complete development of a new CoHousing project presents a CoHousing Group with complex array of tasks to carry out and a multitude of different roles that will need to be undertaken.

This range of activities and involvements is likely to present demands to meet at least some of all the following kinds of work:

Group development - how a Group builds up a strong and cohesive identity that can mobilise action meet its ambitions.

Group training - how a Group identifies the various skills required of its members and what it does to achieve this.

Property Development - satisfying the multitude of tasks required by any modern residential development project.

Financial Appraisals - keeping track of the total funds required to make the property development happen, and then paying for it.

Project Management - actively managing a clear sequence of requirements though all stages of the project's life.

Community development - how a Group uses all the above activity and energy to the lasting benefit of a strong community mentality.

Put together, all of these elements require some kind of methodological approach to identify separate and successive requirements of a project's key tasks and goals at various stages of its intended development.

Any such methodological approach needs to be able to recognise tasks essential to a project's ultimate success from merely those that could be desirable. It should be able to focus the attention of CoHousing Groups upon what must be secured in order for their overall progress to be secured.

Furthermore, there is a need for a 'framework' against which all the various elements of a project's development can be assessed and monitored. This is not a dry obligation from our audit-obsessed age, but a crucial tool that is vital for groups to understand what needs to be done next to progress their project's success, and who is to carry out the tasks required to deliver this success.

A format for considering the overall requirements of CoHousing business has been laid out below. For the sake of making subsequent comments easier to digest, this format has been given a structure with four distinct periods or stages of a scheme's overall development. The stages are not in any way sacrosanct in themselves, and it may certainly be thought that other 'divisions' can make as much sense as the suggestions here. The point of making some divisions between the different tasks is not, however, merely for academic debate - rather it should be seen as a definite means of a group being able to assess it's real level of progress. The 'stages' should therefore be seen as representing a proposed means of evaluating the timing at which key decisions ought to have been agreed and taken, and the attendant activities may be expected to have been carried out. These stages of a CoHousing community's development can be summarised as :

Stage One.
Consolidating a CoHousing group's aspirations - when the Project takes on a real independent identity

Stage Two.
Confirming CoHousing development partnerships - when the Group must be clear what is needed to deliver success

Stage Three.
Co-ordinating the CoHousing development on-site - when the actual building works are delivered

Stage Four.
Commencing life within the new neighbourhood - when the Community's ambitions have at last materialised

Below each stage has been provided with a set of

comments that are focused upon a sequence of main 'goals' and 'tasks' that will shape peoples' confidence that their project's development is being addressed appropriately. Comment has been provided on how each of these tasks can impact both upon the accumulative progress of the project and upon the cohesion of the intended community as a living whole.

Over and above this sequential description of tasks, the comments are deliberately presented within the framework of a Business Plan, with much emphasis on how such planning relates to a modern construction project. It is in the nature of how any CoHousing project will be addressing residential development issues that this mindset is to what CoHousing groups will need to adopt. Groups will need to regard themselves as a form of housing 'developer' and conduct their business in a relevant and appropriate manner.

For many existing CoHousing groups in the UK, the intention to develop a CoHousing neighbourhood will inevitably involve a group in having to win over various hearts-and-minds in support of its aspirations. This will itself entail the need for the group to be clear about how the group plans to approach the complementary but different elements and stages of its project. A summary is therefore provided of the kinds of topics that groups should consider within their formal presentations of their 'Plan' - i.e. how they shape the marketing of their ambitions.

A list is then provided as a suggested point for CoHousing Groups to still spend some time of a consideration of what will be the immediate flavour of their neighbourhood community life when the project has delivered its buildings and households are in occupation. Suggestions have been made for the first neighbourhood policies a Group may wish to put into place in order to make the transition from aspiring community to real neighbourhood as smooth as possible.

Sequential tasks in CoHousing development

The following pages lists an Outline Summary of the main CoHousing development tasks that groups should consider and advice on what could require consideration or further action(s), by way of satisfying 'key issues to consider' and the potential 'impact upon Group cohesion'.

Groups can add or subtract from these lists as befit the individual character of their project's stages of achievement and resources. A sensible approach to such project development could be to assume that all the tasks suggested will be required by a project. A group can then find in its own time that it has met the necessary demands of that part of the development process, rather than be impatient for progress and overlook what could prove damaging to project delivery at some time in the future and weaken overall cohesion.

STAGE ONE TASKS
Initiation and consolidation of Group aspirations

- Initial formation of CoHousing group and recruitment of members
- Identifying core aspirations and vision building
- Setting clear aims and objectives
- Agree decision-making process and conflict resolution
- Initial agreement for formal identity of group and start implementation
- Summarise immediate resources and review tasks and roles of group members
- Produce promotional summary of group vision and progress
- Agree process for members leaving the group
- Miscellaneous :
  Arrange meetings and social events
  Decide on role and degree of fund-raising
  Treasurer duties

STAGE TWO TASKS
Confirming development partnerships

- Identify need for potential Partners:
- Appointing agents / partners
- Clarifying terms for 'working capital'
- Conduct comprehensive site / properties search

- Review 'parameter' agreement(s) of group
- Review 'options' to acquire site(s)
- Consider abstract / sketch development options for identified site(s)
- Review requirement to produce formal Business Plan on paper
- Review tasks and roles of group members

STAGE THREE TASKS
Co-ordinating site development

- Agree terms for acquisition of identified site(s)
- Agree terms of finance
- Clarify timetable of funds required from members
- Confirm role of agents to draw up plans
- Group to agree key design criteria
- Clarify 'in principle' criteria and timetable for allocation of properties
- Review finances required from members
- Agree final specification(s)/ dimensions / format of Building Works / and construction tender process / on-site roles 'in principle'
- Tender and appointment of Construction Team
- Agree timetable for construction and building works
- Management of Construction period
- Review tasks and roles of group members

STAGE FOUR TASKS
Commencement of new neighbourhood

- Procedure for final payment of project expenses
- Handover of property to group
- Final requirements for finances from group members
- Handover Procedure to individual households
- Clarify any final changes in group membership
- Clarify first 'neighbourhood policies' for living as a communal neighbourhood
- Confirm new tasks & roles for community members

STAGE ONE	Consolidation of Group aspirations
CORE TASK OR ACTIONS	**CORE ISSUES TO BE SATISIFIED**
Initial CoHousing Group formation	When are the first people sufficient to take on informal identity of a 'group'?
Identify core aspirations	Acceptable size of project Acceptable or target tenure(s) Range of location possibilities Range of facilities on-site Facilities in neighbourhood Potential personal investment of time / DIY / self-build / etc
Summary of Group Vision	An initial but clear statement on what the group represents and what it is seeking to achieve. through a CoHousing scheme.

Summarise immediate resources	<u>Finance:</u> Available capital
	        Estimate of Income
	        Estimate of other funds
	<u>Land / opportunities</u>
	Available sites or buildings
	Options for sites etc.
	<u>Skills :</u>Identification of these
	Learning new ones
	Sharing between members
	Assessing shortfalls & considering future acquisitions

Procedures for decision-making and resolving conflict	Basic clarity on how the group reaches and records its decisions is vital to a healthy dynamic of the community.
Initial agreement on formal legal identity	[Consider issues in section on the range of potential legal identities.]
Produce material for promotion	This is to be an initial printed summary of Group progress
Review tasks & roles of Group members	Clarify the any key roles and tasks that need to be undertaken or regularised in order to consolidate all the above issues.

KEY CONSIDERATIONS	ISSUES FOR PROJECT COHESION
Agreement needed for frequency of meetings, record-keeping, means of reaching decisions, reaching agreement	Groups can linger too long at the very initial stage - momentum from carrying out other tasks will attract interest from potential members.
Groups need to be as clear about what they could accept & what they would not. Some members may have an 'ideal', - however just as important is what could be acceptable if only part of that 'ideal' was realised.	Be clear and precise on the minimum the group will accept, but then accept the possibility of this 'minimum' being the shape of a future solution - having a minimum that people then reject is not a workable minimum.
Be precise. This will be the group's first "calling card" to the other bodies with whom a Group is likely to be dealing. Make contact with other projects and with sources of acknowledged experience, but be prepared to pay for some personal advice.	Try and agree a group discipline for what initial 'opportunities' will be followed up in support of this vision. Don't change the core vision just to suit suitors or potential partners, but be aware of how such a vision relates to the other's usual world-view.
Agree criteria for deciding sufficient or necessary resources for scheme progress, and clarify which of these are realistic already within the group, and which will be required through other bodies / formal agents.	Groups may have members with relevant backgrounds to some key tasks. It may not be viable to use those skills in lieu of formal agents (such as an architect) It may introduce friction & weakness into the groups dynamic. Better to discuss how those skills can help resource an evaluation of an agent's work.
Clear decision-making will help make sense of competing priorities..	Training for dealing with potential conflict will help promote positive expectations.
Try & limit the time given to the deliberation of a group's constitution & plans for legal registration.	Use the suggested legal formats in the Appendix to save time & effort. future registrations can follow.
This should contain an initial summary of the group's progress.	Use 'core aspirations' already identified to shape the group's image.
Groups need to clarify what is reasonable to expect as its business. E.g. if childcare is not the group's responsibility, this need not appear as a task.	Share the group's responsibilities between all group members.

STAGE TWO	Confirming development partnerships
CORE TASK OR ACTIONS	**CORE ISSUES TO BE SATISIFIED**
Identification of agents / potential partners	Groups need to consider how their project will require working relationships with the following: Owners of key land or property Solicitor / Legal support Designer / Architect /Engineer Housebuilders Landscape Architect
Appointing agents / agreeing partners	Use an interview & appointment process to secure appropriately skilled bodies. Clarify the basis of core services required, to be provided and the fees for this. Clarify agent's commitments on time/ availability/resources, and which personnel would carry out tasks
Clarify need for initial 'working capital'	Determine estimates & agreements of what funds may be required by members to meet initial expenses (e.g. auctions, site investigations).
Active site search	Start strategic and methodical search for sites or suitable properties
Finalise Group's 'parameters' for accepting a site	A minimum clarity is required of the types of site and geographical areas that will interest a group, and on what will not.
Review 'options' to acquire site(s)	Consider options and costs to declare formal interest for purchasing site(s) in future
Abstract / sketch development options	Consider first role of agent to sketch development options for identified site(s)
Formal 'Business Plan'	Review production of a formal Business Plan to promote project and acquire necessary support or resources
Review tasks & roles of Group members	Review key roles and tasks to consolidate all the above issues and prepare for next stage.

KEY CONSIDERATIONS	ISSUES FOR PROJECT COHESION
An agent engaged to act on a group's behalf (and paid by them) will be different from a potential partner who may support the project through other means. Partners could assist in acquiring finance, or provide land by fitting CoHousing in a wider housing development - agents will be those who skills help the group satisfy key tasks.	Use agents that are capable of supporting the group's aspirations with experience of work with community-led projects.
Always interview bodies for all positions. See suggested sets of 'interview' questions in previous chapters Be clear about what some form of 'partnership' could offer the partners a group may court, and be direct in promoting this	Contact agents referees - clarify what was required by them and what was delivered. Consider a visit to a key example of a designer's work. A full interview will be an investment to help any future debate on performance.
If the project is for a mix of tenures, & not all members have the opportunity to raise much capital, consider alternative financesources.	Clarify what happens to the working capital of members who may wish to leave the group during project development.
Acknowledge the requirement to act quickly for some sales -e.g. what to do to meet auction deadlines.	Info on sites will be in a range of places (agencies, developers, trade press) share search work out.
It is crucial to clarify if some members are 'holding out' for just one kind of development (e.g. like a greenfield eco-project).	Some sites will be more attractive to some members than to others, the group needs confidence to act on sites meeting the minimum.
Groups need to acquire detail of other agreement to acquire an 'option' for site(s) identified as basis for any negotiations.	Fully discuss cost of acquiring formal 'option' on a site in terms of buying time to secure other necessary resources.
Be realistic on what an 'outline' sketch of a site can provide if attempting to limit agent's cost.	Include all potential tenure(s) within the sketch options.
See section on content of proposed Plan - especially detail of 'essentials' and 'desirables'.	Agree clear budget for production of Plan and obtain a number of quotes from printers

STAGE THREE Co-ordinating site development	
CORE TASK OR ACTIONS	**CORE ISSUES TO BE SATISIFIED**
Finalise terms for acquisition of identified site	Make the terms for the identified site subject (at least for a given period) to the group acquiring full planning permission and the necessary finances.
Finalise terms of finance required of funding bodies	Agree terms and nature of finance required for agreed development option
Clarify timetable of funds from Group	Clarify timetable of funds from group and any criteria for change in membership
Confirm instructions to draw up plans	Formal plans required to seek - planning approval - Building Control approvals
Group agree key design issues	Key design elements to agree - dimensions buildings - dimensions of open spaces - siting of facilities
Final plans to be submitted for formal approvals	Confirm time to be taken by agents and expected timetable of submissions and likely approvals.
Clarify criteria for property allocation	Clarify criteria for 'in principle' allocation of properties on final scheme completion.
Review financial requirements	Review requirements of members, either as working capital or at property handover.
Agree format of process to steer building works as a whole	Process will involve : - final specification(s) in documents - format of Building Works - format of tender process - on-site roles 'in principle'
Tender process	Appointment of any main builder Appointment of additional site agents
Clarify timetable for construction	Agree overall timetable for construction and building works
Management of on-site construction period	Clarify management of construction period for: - work & roles of agents / contractors - on-site liaison(s) / meetings / decisions - timing of payments and funds required - quality control-information to partners
Review tasks & roles	Review roles & tasks to be undertaken

KEY CONSIDERATIONS	ISSUES FOR PROJECT COHESION
Consider use of an agent to finalise these terms, if the group is not experienced in such matters. Look at examples of legal agreements	Partnership with a developer on a large site will seem different from a stand-alone site, however core issues are still pertinent.
Main funding will most likely be as a form of development loan from the private sector.	Ensure overall proposals do not place households at risk of funds being removed in future.
Confirm basis on receiving funds in whole or in part from members	Confirm basis for returning funds to ex-members, if change occurs.
Clarify how members can best liaise with agents - as a whole or via dedicated sub-group.	Be clear on likely timetable of preparing plans and time taken to receive formal approvals.
The siting of the shared facilities and the common building will be crucial to promoting a 'community' ethos.	Clarify priorities for design dimensions and accept limitations of actual site if not all designs can be made to work.
If plans are to go to a local planning committee, then request to make a presentation in person.	Set limits to how long any amendments from group members will be accepted.
Separate wish to allocate immediately from principles of how allocations can be made.	Try and identify impact upon any future service charges for spaces / equipment / etc.
The group needs to be clear how the requirements will relate to all members' incomes.	Agree ways to decide between households interested in same units and their fall-back choice
Include within the overall format the role of the group to attend site meetings, as well as how it will consider the nature of works in progress in its own meetings.	Draw all members' attention to any key design issues or budget limitations that are detailed in the project's works specification.
Clarify any self-build / DIY intentions to agents	Restrict the enthusiasm to save money by doing on-site work.
Co-ordinate works timetable with having finance available.	Be clear on the main possibilities for potential delay.
Clarify how members liaise with builders. A dedicated sub-group will be most feasible during on-site hours, however plan other meetings to share perspectives and information on the emerging buildings.	Clarify requirements for group meetings and ongoing dynamics whilst works in progress.

CORE TASK OR ACTIONS	CORE ISSUES TO BE SATISIFIED
Completion of formal contracts and costs	Procedure for final payments of project expenses
Property handover to Group	Handover of completed property to whole group
Clarify final membership of new community	Clarify any final changes in group membership
Finalise format of members payments	Clarify requirement and absolute last moment for final finances from group members.
Property handover to members	Procedure of handover to individual member households
Confirm first neighbourhood policies'	Clarify first policies & agreements for living as a communal neighbourhood.
Confirm new tasks and roles of community members	Review aspirations for roles and tasks that need to be undertaken in new neighbourhood

Format of a CoHousing Business Plan

The successful creation of a new intended neighbourhood community is obviously more important than what is written into any formal Plan. Having a formal Plan is, however, a fundamental means whereby a group will be able to communicate its ambitions and methods and to demonstrate a Group's readiness to plan ahead and to act decisively.

A key function of a Business Plan for CoHousing Development will be to present a picture of the intended CoHousing project to potential supporters or stakeholders - in particular to potential financial partners. A Plan that has been competently constructed and well-presented will enhance a CoHousing group's reputation and strengthen the likelihood of the group meeting its objectives. A Plan that is

KEY CONSIDERATIONS	ISSUES FOR PROJECT COHESION
Ensure funds available are sufficient to cover last-minute extra requirements.	Give full breakdown of all final costs to all members within draft legal papers.
Is handover of properties likely to be in phases?	Phased occupation can address concerns for site security, but a cost can be unequal cohesion to developing between neighbours.
Agree any revisions to formal procedures for members joining or leaving the Group.	Clarify if there is a pressing need for ownership or rental members
Complete legal frameworks for transfer or use of properties to individual households.	Clarify expectations for level of any service charges and procedures for payment.
Adhere to initial principles for property allocations, raised at Stage Three.	Should be prior to members move-in (even if DIY intentions for members to finish interiors).
[See below for potential topics.]	Discussions before occupation will help avoid conflicts from unvoiced expectations.
Agree immediate terms and expectations for members' use of common building.	Encourage use of common building to cement new and regular connections between neighbours.

poorly constructed, however, will be easily damaging to the group's reputation, particularly in the view of those stakeholders who have the scope or position to influence the group's future.

It is fairly common for Business Plans to indicate the new activity that is being promoted - for example, the intended development of new community and housing resources - yet be lacking in providing much detail of exactly how this activity is to be achieved. Any such lack of detail in explaining how the project's ambitions and strategy are to be implemented represent a fundamental weakness, and will create a major barrier to conveying a group's ambition to their intended audience.

Stutley (2001, p39) has noted 10 reasons why formal Business Plans can fail to carry out this basis role:

1. The presentation of the Plan appears false, as it is either too scruffy or too slick.

2. The length of the text is too long, and is full of generalisations and waffle.

3. The text is too short and too vague.

4. There are insufficient facts and details for what is being proposed.

5. There are actual factual errors in the text.

6. There are clear omissions to the presentation that suggest necessary skills or resources are lacking.

7. There is insufficient consideration or analysis of 'what if...?' situations (e.g. 'what if costs are underestimated?'; 'what if interest rates rise?').

8. The overall financial projections are unreasonably optimistic.

9. The Plan appears more designed to raise finance than to organise the actual delivery of the project.

10. The Plan was obviously produced by professional consultants, thereby raising doubt on the capability of the project's own management skills.

Within any formal crafting of a CoHousing Business Plan, certain sections and matters are fundamental and unavoidable to it providing a full and appropriate presentation of the CoHousing Group's intentions. These may be called crucial to the Plan's makeup and content. Other matters will assist in filling out this picture, but are arguably less essential, and may thereby be classed as desirable elements of a Plan. This can be indicated by the following summaries:

ELEMENTS THAT WILL BE CRUCIAL TO A BUSINESS PLAN

- Vision and Objectives of the overall project
- Executive Summary of the Business Plan
- Statement on the relationship of the CoHousing project to the wider environment
- General background detail of people to whom the CoHousing project will provide
- Analysis of demand and interest in CoHousing
- Summary of property and facilities in the proposed CoHousing neighbourhood
- Intended process to implement the CoHousing project and projected timetable
- Project investment plan and asset management of CoHousing neighbourhood
- Performance targets for project completion
- Performance monitoring and operational management of built neighbourhood
- Financial/budgetary forecasts, and income projections
- Risk assessments
- Contingency plans

ELEMENTS THAT WILL BE DESIRABLE IN A BUSINESS PLAN

- Brief Statement from the CoHousing organisation
- History of the CoHousing project
- Operational infrastructure - how the CoHousing organisation carries out its business, role of sub-groups, etc.

- Details of loan and borrowing strategies of members

- Peer comparisons with other community-based residential projects

- Governance structure of the CoHousing organisation (legal format, etc.)

- Other internal aspects of CoHousing organisation's operations (IT, HR,)

- Statutory, financial and other obligations

Stutley prompts the designers of Business Plans to be extremely self-critical in evaluating their Plans in terms of the following points -

Does the summary of a Plan provide sufficient information for the reader who will not wade through every page?

Does the flow of the text give sufficient detail of how the Plan's objectives will be achieved?

Is the detail provided on crucial financial matters consistent with the other detail of the text?

Do the financial forecasts in the Plan demonstrate that the Plan's promoters can cope with changing circumstances and other unexpected events?

Living as a communal neighbourhood

Any new CoHousing community will be well-served in spending some time before taking up occupation of the residential properties to think ahead about how everyday life might operate in the new neighbourhood.

There is plenty of advice from existing CoHousing communities on what has been useful for members to clarify their expectations of life in the new environment [see Bibliography for website information].

The list below is not exhaustive in any way, but is provided as one suggestion for the immediate kinds of issues that a new neighbourhood community may quickly need to discuss:

- The arrangement of regular residents' meetings
- The regularity of different meetings
- On-going decision-making (and voting procedures if required)
- If there are fees or costs for the use (or hire?) of neighbourhood facilities
- The conduct of, and responsibility for, visitors and other family members
- Dealing with concerns about noise or other disturbances
- Procedures for acceptance / selection (& induction?) of new members
- Procedures for re-valuation of any service charges
- Arrangements for communal or community activities (e.g. shared meals)
- Arrangements for the cleaning of communal facilities
- Arrangements to look after outside / garden areas
- Garden maintenance, particularly planting of trees and large bushes
- Proximity of play and sports activity in relation to rest of neighbourhood
- Presence of pets and animals
- The parking of cars, bikes, trailers, etc.
- Procedures for dealing with waste/rubbish/recycling

Training and support checklist

Stage of Project Development	Professional support needed
1. Consolidation of Group aspirations	
Initial CoHousing Group formation	
Identify core aspirations and Vision of project	
Agree procedures for decision-making	
Initial agreement on formal legal identity	
Summarise immediate resources	
Produce material for promotion	
Agree process for members leaving the group	
Review next tasks and roles of Group members	
2. Confirming development partnerships	
Identification of agents / potential partners	
Appointing agents and finding partners	
Clarify need for initial 'working capital'	
Conduct methodical site search	
Agree minimum parameters for acceptable sites	
Review 'options' to acquire feasible site(s)	
Sketch outline possibilities for identified site(s)	
Complete formal 'Business Plan'	
Review next tasks and roles of group members	
3. Co-ordinating site development	
Finalise terms for identified site	
Finalise terms of finance from funding bodies	
Timetable of funds required from members	
Confirm role of agent(s) to prepare full plans	
Group agree key design issues with agents	
Submit final plans for formal approvals	
Agree in principle allocation of properties	
Review finance required of members	

We can do it with training and support	We can do it ourselves with training	We can do it without training

Training and support checklist

Stage of Project Development	Professional support needed
3. Co-ordinating site development (Cont'd)	
Tender process - appoint Construction Team	
Finalise construction timetable/building process	
Management of construction period	
Review next tasks and roles of group members	
4. Commencement of new neighbourhood	
Implement final payments to cover project costs	
Property handover to whole group	
Confirm final membership of Group (if required)	
Finalise format of members payments	
Property handovers to member households	
Clarify first 'neighbourhood policies'	
Review procedures for decision-making	
Confirm any new tasks for new neighbourhood	

We can do it with training and support	We can do it our-selves with training	We can do it without training

Chris Coates & Steve Smith have both been involved in working for some years with community groups, self build and other housing initiatives and other eco-building projects. Chris is currently a freelance project development manager and Steve works with the Neighbourhood Initiatives Foundation and on other consultancy projects.

Conclusions

As noted by the detailed description of CoHousing given at the start of this book, it is clear there is still confusion about CoHousing's key attributes, when comparing or contrasting these with other approaches to neighbourhood development. Too often descriptions of CoHousing attempt to explain its features in term of being something else, rather than highlighting where it is significantly different to other forms of modern residential settings. CoHousing's supporters need to be precise and up-front about its character, so that what it offers to UK aspirations for community cohesion can be properly understood. There may be an irrefutable requirement for community members to invest much of themselves into their neighbourhood's development - obvious from reading about the Community Project, and impressive in other ways in the new buildings appearing at Stroud. The ability of this approach to meet communal aspirations has, however, so much to offer those looking at modern scenarios for 'sustainable' community and reinforcing social capital.

Jydstrup Savverk Sealand Denmark

The chapter describing ideas on CoHousing for Older People encapsulates a very live issue within current debate on public policy - namely how to address concerns that many people may still be bound for 'nursing homes', 'geriatric' wards, or isolating loneliness at home alone, in lieu of

Thundercliffe Grange Nr Rotherham

any other options. Current ideas for alternatives to such a future seem focused upon either reinvigorating people's home-based 'independence' or through providing new accommodation in 'care village' developments, responsive and supportive to a wide range of needs. This last concept is particularly common in ideas for replacing existing sheltered housing accommodation with modern improvements. What is still lacking in such debate is an acknowledgement of contemporary aspirations from groups like OWCH demanding that an emphasis on 'independence and dignity' should include acceptance of Older People's own ideas and desires for collective settings. Indeed, people's insistence that this should promote resident-control and self-determination for older people that would be taken as a natural feature of proposals for other neighbourhood settings! Here CoHousing offers another option for how older people can maintain control over their own lives, while not being isolated from others - i.e. as part of a shared and supportive neighbourhood quite removed from the paternalism still present in other some of the other proposals. Even as a simple alternative to current 'sheltered housing' accommodation, CoHousing can clearly offer itself as a model for a self-managed and stable community, distinct from any risk of compromise required in providing the costly support that is central to the care village approach. The mutual but informal support from CoHousing residents to one another diminishes calls upon other services (usually statutory ones), as each CoHousing community comes to respond to the natural characteristics of its residents in its own time. There should clearly be a cost benefit here, as well as the satisfaction of new ways to meet people's own aspirations!

What cannot be avoided is the realisation of just how complicated and multi-faceted undertaking CoHousing development in the UK will currently be. It is a collective approach

Common house. Amhurst Cohousing Mass. USA

in the midst of a mass of such individualistic values that govern how much of 'housebuilding industry' operates. By that virtue it is presented with a clear requirement that outside agents or partners will need careful courting, and that the likely pace of development will demand much patience, and not a little luck to hear of potential sites just when they could be available! It will be crucial that CoHousing Groups can agree on the main parameters of their collective ambition so that this can channel energies into fruitful endeavour, and not be dissipated by unrealistic longing for a quick solution. Different frameworks exist that can make this endeavour less complicated - Groups should use what experience has been already pulled together by CoHousing's advocates and practitioners. While it will remain important for each community to hold on to its core values, there are finer details in the 'devel-

Thinking About CoHousing

opment process' that will be open to alteration at a later time - not everything must be sorted out before a Group can move a single step forward! Use the Business Plan approach to evaluate how a project could appear to others, as well as identifying what should logically shape the priorities for one's own energies. The emergence of a viable'support infrastructure would be of such advantage here, like the network of professionals that are so supportive of CoHousing in the States - demonstrating a clear regard for resident-led design and development.

The emergence of the new build project in Stroud has certainly demonstrated that new CoHousing development can be achieved where the scheme has access to sufficient private resources - providing a suitable site can be acquired. The current state of the housing market and the exorbitant levels of house and land prices may not be that conducive, however, to this being immediately replicable. The development sector bodies that are used to finding and acquiring sites for development are fast securing monopolies on many future land opportunities. It will therefore seem increasingly likely that access to sites in many areas may demand CoHousing Groups to woo those builders and developers who have already acquired the local sites. While this may seem daunting, the increasing Governmental pressure on housebuilding to include provision for a range of tenures and households actually offers CoHousing the opportunity it is well-positioned to take up. CoHousing's clear strength is its ability to shape a quite intimate setting that can bring together a mix of tenures and households that other development still resists. Where the planning policies for larger development sites are likely to require developers to provide some mix of tenures, CoHousing can already demonstrate straightforward and practical answers to usual concerns about such development - area management, sale values, recreational requirements, open space, to name bit a few.

The current concern for the level of housebuilding that is taking place in the UK has not given sufficient consideration to an examination of what modern neighbourhoods require. A planning for new dwellings needs to embrace more than just considerations of how to supply a sufficient number of dwellings to individual households - a comprehensive approach should also include different aspirations for where those dwellings will be, and what types of community they can support. It is still a concern that large-scale proposals for new

Springhill CoHousing Community. Stroud

housing in the UK, some under the banner of sustainable communities, have still to make the most of continental masterplanning experience that shares the design and development of new communities with the households that will occupy them. The wider ambitions of Government policy and committed bodies like the Princes Foundation are determined to forge the opportunities for new 'communities' to be created. At the macro level this can be a strong and impressive leadership. At the micro street-level, however, households coming together to live in sustainable neighbourhoods should encompass approaches like CoHousing which will provide people with the opportunity to put a shared and solid character upon how actual neighbourhoods will function.

CoHousing is one very simple but clever answer to a host of modern questions - it is time it brought its light out into the open and made more of a name for itself.

This section provides example documents on the formal incorporation of a CoHousing organisation and an agreement of a CoHousing community's principles of existence.

Memorandum & Articles of Association for a CoHousing Company limited by guarantee

These two documents form the constitution of a limited company, as set out under the prescribed detail required under Company law and in the regulations of Company House.

The memorandum describes the essential attributes of the company and its relationship with the world-at-large. It is required to state the name of the company, whether the registered office is to be situated in England or Wales, the objects of the company and the respective liability of its members.

The articles of association regulate the internal organisation and affairs of the company. They determine how the powers conferred on the company by the memorandum of association shall be exercised. The articles cannot confer wider powers than the memorandum. If there is any inconsistency between the two documents, the memorandum prevails and any alteration to the articles which conflicts with the memorandum is void.

The example documents are for a Company Limited by Guarantee, drawn from those originally registered by the CoHousing Communities Foundation [N.B. no longer in existence, but the principles of these model documents remain on file at Company House]. A small amount of additional detail stems from other registrations like the OWCH group in London.

Example: Memorandum & Articles of Association for a CoHousing Company limited by guarantee

MEMORANDUM OF ASSOCIATION OF
"The.....................................CoHousing Company Ltd."

1. The name of the Company is The .... Ltd.

2. The registered office of the Company will be ...., UK

3. The Company is established for public benefit :-

(a) to promote CoHousing as a specifically beneficial form of residential community development in the area of ...., designed and operated to enable the community's residents to live within a self-contained setting which combines private accommodation with other communally-run buildings or services, thereby maximising opportunity for community members to support and interact with one another on a regular basis as the community may decide;

(b) to relieve persons in the area of ....who are in conditions of housing need by reason of their economic circumstances or social isolation, through the provision of facilities to support the development of at least one CoHousing scheme within the ... area and therein improve the quality of such persons' social welfare ;

(c) to promote the advancement of education and learning in relation tohow CoHousing schemes function and are developed, including the development of skills which can assist people to acquire accommodation in a CoHousing setting in the area of ....

(d) to promote other such charitable or not-for-profit purposes for the general public benefit within the area of ..... in order to sustain the ongoing development of local CoHousing communities, as the Company shall think fit;

[PROVIDED that in furtherance of all or any of the above objects the Company shall have the power to promote provide or assist activities outside the area referred to above where it is of the opinion that to do so will benefit the inhabitants of the said area]

And the Company shall have the following powers exercisable in furtheranceof its said objects or any of them but not otherwise namely:

(1) To acquire or secure commissions or other engagements to promote the furtherance of the objects listed above.

(2) To engage with statutory services and other voluntary organisations to set up training and other educational courses for any one or more of the objects of the company.

(3) To promote community businesses, especially those based upon an explicit CoHousing character, which are non-profit making or which employ the whole of their profits for the public benefit and whose objectives and activities are directed towards the provision of paid employment to poor residents of the area of benefit or towards relief for poor residents of the area of benefit or towards other purposes of general public utility and the

acquisition and holding of the shares, stocks, debentures, and other interests in companies whose objectives and activities are so directed and the
provision of managerial, supervisory and consultancy services to or in
respect of such companies.

(4) To supplement and complement (but not replace) existing statutory
services and to co-operate with statutory authorities and voluntary organisations having similar aims.

(5) To purchase, take on lease or in exchange, hire or otherwise acquire any
other real and personal estate which may be deemed necessary or convenient for any objects of the Company.

(6) To construct, maintain, improve, rebuild and alter any houses, buildings
or works necessary for the objects of the Company.

(7) To accept gifts of any property or money including any interest therein,
whether subject to any special trust or not, for any one or more of the
objects of the Company.

(8) To take such steps by personal or written appeals, public meetings or
otherwise as may from time to time be deemed expedient for the purpose
of procuring subscriptions, or otherwise provided that the trustees shall
not undertake any permanent trading activities in raising funds for its charitable objects.

(9) To cause to be written, printed, published and circulated (gratuitously or
otherwise) any newspapers, periodicals, pamphlets, reports, journals, films,
instructional matter, books, recorded tapes, documentsor leaflets and to
organise lectures, classes, exhibitions, meetings, seminars, broadcasts and
courses of instruction necessary for the promotion of its objects, either
alone or with others.

(10) To purchase or otherwise acquire or found and to carry on training
centres.

(11) To foster and undertake research into any aspect of the objects of the
Company and its work and to disseminate the results of such research.

(12) Subject to such consents as may be required by law to sell, manage,
lease, mortgage, charge, insure, dispose of, or otherwise deal with or turn
to account all or any part of the property of the Company.

(13) Subject to such consents as may be required by law to borrow and
raise money for the purposes of the Company in such manner as the
Companymay think fit.

(14)(a) To invest income received by the Company not immediately
required for its purposes in or upon such investments, securities or property of whatever nature and wherever situated or place the same on
deposit at interest with any bank insurance company or local authority as
may be thought fit.
(b) To invest the capital of the Company not immediately required for its
purposes in or upon such investments, securities, land (including any estate
or interest in the same) and property of whatever nature and wherever situated and whether income producing or not including such personal cred-

it with or without security as may be thought fit.

PROVIDED always that the powers in sub-clauses 14(a) and 14(b) shall be exercised subject to such conditions and consents as may from time to time be imposed or required by law and subject also to the provisions here-inafter contained.

(15)To undertake any charitable or not-for-profit trusts which will further any of the objects of the Company.

(16) To employ and/or engage persons for each and any objects and/or pur-poses of the Company and make all reasonable and necessary provisions for the payment of pensions and superannuation benefits to or in respect of employees and their other dependants.

(17) To establish and support, and to aid in the establishment and support of, any other trusts, associations, bodies or corporations wheresoever con-stituted or operating formed exclusively for all or
any of the objects of the Company the establishment or support in aid in the establishment or support of which shall be legally charitable.

(18)To purchase or otherwise acquire and undertake all or any part of the property, assets, liabilities and engagements of any one or more of the com-panies, institutions, societies or associations with which the Company is authorised to amalgamate.

(19) To draw, make, accept, endorse, discount, execute and issue promissory notes, bills, cheques and other instruments and to operate bank accounts.

(20) To insure and arrange insurance cover for and to indemnify its officers, servants and voluntary workers from and against all such risks incurred in the course of the performance of their duties as may be thought fit.

(21) To pay out of the funds of the Company the cost, charges and expens-es of and incidental to the formation of the Company and its registration under the Companies Acts and the Charities Act 1994.

(22)To do all such other lawful things in order to further the attainment of the above objects or any of them

PROVIDED that :
(i) in case the Company shall take or hold any property which may be sub-ject to such trusts, the Company shall only deal with or invest the same in such manner as allowed by law, having regard to such trusts;
(ii) the objects of the Company shall not extend to the regulation or rela-tions between workers and employers or organisations of workers and organisations of employers;
(iii) in case the Company shall take or hold any property subject to the jurisdiction of the Charity Commissioners for England and Wales the Company shall not sell, mortgage, charge or lease the same without such authority, approval or consent as may be required by law, and as regards any such property the Management Committee of the Company shall be chargeable for any such property that may come into their hands and shall be answerable and accountable for their own acts, receipts, neglects and defaults, and for the due administration of such property in the same man-ner and to the same extent as they would as such Management Committee

have been if no incorporation had been effected, and the incorporation of the members shall not diminish or impair any control or authority exercisable by the Chancery Division, or the Charity Commissioners over such Management Committee but they shall as regards any such property be subject jointly and severally to such control or authority as if the Company were not incorporated.

4.The income and property of the Company shall be applied solely towards the promotion of its objects as set forth in this Memorandum of Association and no portion thereof shall be paid or transferred directly or indirectly by way of dividend, bonus or otherwise howsoever by way of profit to members of the Company and no member of its Management Committee shall be appointed to any office of the Company paid by salary or fees, or receive any remuneration or other benefit in money or money's worth from the Company

PROVIDED that nothing herein shall prevent any payment in good faith by the Company:-
(a) of reasonable and proper remuneration to any officer or servant of the Company not being a member of the Management Committee for any services rendered to the Company;
(b) of interest on money lent by any member of the Company or its Management Committee at a rate per annum not exceeding 2% less than the base lending rate prescribed for the time being by a clearing Bank selected by the Management Committee or 3% whichever is the greater;
(c) of reasonable and proper rent for premises demised or let by any member of the Company or of its Management Committee;
(d) of fees, remuneration or other benefits in money or money's worth to a company of which a member of the Management Committee may be a member holding not more than 1/100 part of the capital of that company;
(e) to any member of its Management Committee of reasonable out-of-pocket expenses.

5.The liability of the members is limited.

6.Every member of the Company undertakes to contribute to the assets of the Company, in the event of the same being wound up while s/he is a member, or within one year after s/he ceases to be a member, for payment of the debts and liabilities of the Company contracted before s/he ceases to be a member, and of the costs, charges and expenses of winding up, and for the adjustment of the rights of the contributories among themselves, such amount as may be required not exceeding one pound.

7.If upon the winding up or dissolution of the Company there remains, after the satisfaction of all its debts and liabilities, any property whatsoever, the same shall not be paid to or distributed among the members of the Company, but shall be given or transferred to some other charitable institution or institutions, having objects similar to the objects of the Company, and which shall prohibit the distribution of its or their income and property among its or their members to an extent at least as great as is imposed on the Company under or by virtue of Clause 4 hereof, such institution or institutions to be determined by the members of the Company at or before the time of dissolution, and if and so far as effect cannot be given to such provision then to some charitable object.

ARTICLES OF ASSOCIATION OF
"THE ....CoHOUSING COMPANY LTD"

INTERPRETATION

1.   In these Articles:
     "the Act' means the Companies Act 1985.
     "the Seal" means the common seal of the Company.
     "Company Secretary" means any person appointed to
     perform the duties of the secretary of the Company.
      "the United Kingdom" means Great Britain & Northern Ireland.
     "the Management Committee" means the Management
     Committee for the time being.

Expressions referring to writing shall, unless the contrary intention appears, be construed as including references to printing, lithography, photography, and other modes of representing or reproducing words in a visible form.

Unless the context otherwise requires, words or expressions contained in these Articles shall bear the same meaning as in the Act or \ any statutory modification thereof in force at the date at which these Articles become binding on the Company.

2. The Company is established for the purposes expressed in the Memorandum of Association of the Company PROVIDED that no amendment shall be made either to the Memorandum of Association of the Company or to these Articles which shall cause the Company to lose the status of a charity at law.

3. The Company is incorporated under the Companies Act 1985 as a company limited by guarantee and not having a share capital.

II   MEMBERS
4. The number of Members with which the Company proposes to be registered is …….. but the Management Committee may from time to time register an increase of Members.

5. The Subscribers to the Memorandum of Association and such other persons as the Management Committee shall admit to Membership (subject nevertheless to the provisions of Articles 6 and 70(a) hereof) shall be Members of the Company.

6. Any person shall be admitted to membership upon receipt by the Company Secretary of a signed application in writing in a form to be approved by the Management Committee stating that such person approves the objects and general principles and aims of the Company as herein before set out unless the Management Committee shall within six weeks of such receipt decide that in their view (which decision shall be final) the admission of the applicant to membership would be prejudicial to the interests of the Company.

7. Each individual member shall pay a subscription of not less than £..... in each financial year
PROVIDED that the respective amounts of such subscriptions may be increased from time to time in accordance with Article 70 hereof.

8. A member shall cease to be a member in the following circumstances:

(i) if such member's subscription shall not be paid within one month after the end of the financial year unless the Management Committee shall in its absolute discretion otherwise decide;

(ii) if guilty of such conduct as in the opinion of the Management Committee shall be at variance with the objects and principles of the Company, be prejudicial to its interests, or be in breach of the Company's Rules and Bye-laws - in which case she can be expelled from the Membership by a General Meeting of the Company by a vote of 60% of the Membership, provided that any Member whose expulsion is to be considered shall have the right to make a representation to the meeting at which the question is to be decided and that the notices calling the meeting specify that the question of such expulsion is to be raised; or

iii) if such member gives notice in writing to the Company Secretary at the registered office of the Company of her/his intention to retire from membership.

III   GENERAL MEETINGS

9. The Company shall in each year hold a General Meeting as its Annual General Meeting in addition to any other meetings in that year, and shall specify the meeting as such in the notices calling it; and not more than fifteen months shall elapse between the date of one Annual General Meeting of the Company and that of the next provided that so long as the Company holds its first Annual General Meeting within eighteen months of its incorporation, it need not hold it in the year of its incorporation or in the following year. The Annual General Meeting shall be held at such time and place as the Management Committee shall appoint.

10. All General Meetings other than Annual General Meetings shall be called Extraordinary General Meetings.

11. The Management Committee may, whenever they think fit, convene an Extraordinary General Meeting. Extraordinary General Meetings may also be convened at the request of ..... members or 66% [sixty six per cent] of the members of the Company, whichever is the greater.

12. An Annual General Meeting and a meeting called for the passing of a special resolution shall be called by giving at least twenty-one days' clear notice in writing. Meetings of the Company other than an Annual General Meeting shall be called by giving at least fourteen days' clear notice in writing. The notice shall specify the place, date, and time of the meeting and the general nature of any special business to be discussed. Notice of the meeting must be given to everyone entitled to receive such notices under these Articles,

PROVIDED that a meeting of the Company shall, notwithstanding that it is called by shorter notice than that specified in this Article, be deemed to have been duly called if it is so agreed:-

(a) in the case of a meeting called as the Annual General Meeting, by all the

Members entitled to attend and vote thereat; and

(b) in the case of any other meeting, by a majority in number of the Members having a right to attend and vote at the meeting, being a majority together representing not less than ninety-five per cent of the total voting rights at that meeting of all the Members.

13. The accidental omission to give notice of a meeting to, or the non-receipt of notice of a meeting by, any person entitled to receive notice shall not invalidate the proceedings at that meeting.

IV   PROCEEDINGS AT GENERAL MEETINGS

14. All business shall be deemed special that is transacted at an Extraordinary General Meeting, and also all that is transacted at an Annual General Meeting, with the exception of the consideration of the accounts, balance sheets, and the reports of the Management Committee and auditors, the election of members of the Management Committee in the place of those retiring and the appointment of, and the fixing of the remuneration of, the auditors.

15. No business shall be transacted at any General Meeting unless a quorum of Members is present at the time when the meeting proceeds to business. Save as otherwise provided in these Articles the lesser of 10 [ten] or 25% [twenty five per cent] of the Members present in person or by proxy (or, being a corporate member, by representative) shall be a quorum.

16. If within half an hour from the time appointed for the meeting a quorum is not present, the meeting, if convened upon the requisition of Members, shall be dissolved; in any other case it shall stand adjourned to the same day in the next week, at the same time and place, or to such other day and at such other time and place as the Management Committee may determine, and if at the adjourned meeting a quorum is not present within half an hour from the timeappointed for the meeting the Members present shall be a quorum.

17. Subject to the provisions of the Act, a Resolution in writing signed by all the Members for the time being entitled to receive notice of and to attend and vote on General Meetings (or being corporations, by their duly authorised representatives) shall be as valid and effective as if the same had been passed at a General Meeting of the Company duly convened and held. Such Resolution may consist of several documents in like form each signed by one or more of the Members.

18. The Chair of the Management Committee (or in her/his absence the Vice-Chair, the Honorary Committee Secretary or the Honorary Treasurer in that order) shall preside as Chair at every General Meeting of the Company. If no such person shall be present within fifteen minutes after the time appointed for the holding of the meeting or, if present, no such person is willing to act the Members of the Management Committee present shall elect one of their number to be Chair of the meeting.

19. If at any meeting no Member of the Management Committee is willing to act as Chair or if no Member of the Management Committee is present within fifteen minutes after the time appointed for holding the meeting, the Members present shall choose one of their number to be Chair of the

meeting.

20. The Chair may, with the consent of any meeting at which a quorum is present (and shall if so directed by the meeting), adjourn the meeting from time to time and from place to place, but no business shall be transacted at any adjourned meeting other than the business left unfinished at the meeting from which the adjournment took place. When a meeting is adjourned for thirty days or more, notice of the adjourned meeting shall be given as in the case of an original meeting. Save as aforesaid it shall not be necessary to give any notice of an adjournment or of the business to be transacted at an adjourned meeting.

21. At any General Meeting a resolution put to the vote of the meeting shall be decided on a show of hands unless a poll is (before or on the declaration of the result of the show of hands) demanded:

(a) by the Chair; or

(b) by at least two Members present in person; or

(c) by any Member or Members present in person or by proxy and representing not less than one-tenth of the total voting rights of all the Members having the right to vote at the meeting.

Unless a poll be so demanded a declaration by the Chair that a resolution has on a show of hands been carried or carried unanimously, or by a particular majority, or lost and an entry to that effect in the book containing the minutes of proceedings of the Company shall be conclusive evidence of the fact without proof of the number or proportion of the votes recorded in favour of or against such resolution.

The demand for a poll may be withdrawn.

22. Except as provided in Article 24, if a poll is duly demanded it shall be taken in such manner as the Chair directs, and the result of the poll shall be deemed to be the resolution of the meeting at which the poll was demanded.

23. In the case of an equality of votes, whether on a show of hands or on a poll, the Chair of the meeting at which the show of hands takes place or at which the poll is demanded, shall be entitled to a second or casting vote.

24. A poll demanded on the election of a Chair, or on a question of adjournment, shall be taken forthwith. A poll demanded on any other question shall be taken at such time as the Chair of the meeting directs, and any business other than that upon which a poll has been demanded may be proceeded with pending the taking of the poll.

V   VOTES

25. Every Member shall have one vote.

26. A Member of unsound mind, or in respect of whom an order has been made by any court having jurisdiction in lunacy, may vote, whether on a show of hands or on a poll, by her/his committee, receiver or curator bonis or other person in the nature of a committee, receiver or curator bonis appointed by that court, and any such committee, receiver, curator bonis or other person may, on a poll, vote by proxy.

27. No Member shall be entitled to vote at any General Meeting unless all moneys presently payable by her/him to the Company have been paid.

28. On a poll votes may be given either personally or by proxy.

29. The instrument appointing a proxy shall be in writing under the hand of the appointor or of her/his attorney duly authorised in writing. A proxy need not be a Member of the Company.

30. The instrument appointing a proxy and the power of attorney or other authority, if any, under which it is signed or a notarially certified copy of that power or authority shall be deposited at the registered office of the Company or at such other place within the United Kingdom as is specified for that purpose in the notice convening the meeting, at any time before the time for holding the meeting or adjourned meeting at which the person named in the instrument proposes to vote, or, in the case of a poll, at any time before the time appointed for the taking of the poll, and in default the instrument of proxy shall not be treated as valid.

31. An instrument appointing a proxy shall be in the following form or a form as near thereto as circumstances admit:

      "THE .... LTD."
      I/We
      of
      in the county of   ,
      being a Member/Members of the above named Company,
      hereby appoint
      of
      or failing her/him,
      of
      as my/our proxy to vote for me/us on my/our behalf at the
Annual or Extraordinary, as the case may be/General
Meeting of the Company to be held on day of
      and at any adjournment thereof.

      Signed this   day of

32. Where it is desired to afford Members an opportunity of voting for or against a resolution the instrument appointing a proxy shall be in the following form or a form as near thereto as circumstances admit :
      "THE .... LTD."
      I(We of
      in the county of   ,
      being a Member/Members of the above named Company,
      hereby appoint
      of
      or failing her/him,
      of
      as my/our proxy to vote for me/us on my/our behalf at the/
Annual or Extraordinary, as the case may be/General

Meeting of the Company to be held on day of   19 and at   a n y
adjournment thereof.

Signed this   day of

This form is to be used in favour or against the resolution.
(*Strike out whichever is not desired.)

Unless otherwise instructed, the proxy will vote as s/he thinks fit.

33. The instrument appointing a proxy shall be deemed to confer authority
to demand or join in demanding a poll.

34. A vote given in accordance with the terms of an instrument of proxy
shall be valid notwithstanding the previous death or insanity of the principal or revocation of the proxy or of the authority under which the proxy
was executed, provided that no intimation in writing of such death, insanity or revocation as aforesaid shall have been received by the Company at
the registered office before the commencement of the meeting or
adjourned meeting at which the proxy is used.

VI MANAGEMENT COMMITTEE

35(a) The number of members of the Management Committee shall not be
less than .... nor more than .....

(b) A member of the Management Committee shall be required to be a
member of the Company.

(c) The first members of the Management Committee shall be the subscribers to the Memorandum of Association who shall serve for a period
expiring at the end of the first Annual General Meeting of the Company.

(d) The first members of the Management Committee shall use their best
endeavours to appoint 3 [three] further members as soon as possible, all
of whom shall serve for a period expiring at the end of the first Annual
General Meeting of the Company.

(e) The vacancies arising on the expiration of the aforesaid first terms of
office of the members of the Management Committee referred to in
Articles (c) and (d) above, shall be filled by election by the members of the
Company at the first Annual General Meeting. 50% of the persons so elected shall each serve for a period expiring at the end of the second Annual
General Meeting after their election; the other 50% so elected shall each
serve for a period expiring at the end of the first Annual General Meeting
after their election. The procedure shall thereafter apply that all elections
to fill the subsequent rotational vacancies shall be on the basis that each
person so elected shall serve for a period expiring at the end of the second Annual General Meeting after their election.

(f) Members of the Management Committee retiring pursuant to any of the provisions in these Articles shall be eligible for re-election or re-appointment.

(g)If no eligible and willing person is available at the time of anyAnnual General Meeting to fill any vacancy on the Management
Committee or if any vacancy arises between Annual General Meetings the Management Committee may itself fill such vacancy to serve until the end of the next Annual General Meeting when an election shall be held to fill the vacancy for the balance of the respective term of office.

(h)No paid worker of the Company shall be eligible to serve as a member of the Management Committee.

36.The Members of the Management Committee may be paid all reasonable travelling, hotel and other out-of-pocket expenses   properly incurred by them in attending and returning from meetings
of the Management Committee or any committee thereof or General Meetings or in connection with the activities of the Company.

VII BORROWING POWERS

37. The Management Committee may exercise all the powers of the Company to borrow money and to mortgage or charge its undertaking and property or any part thereof, and to issue debentures, debenture stock, and other securities whether outright or as security for any debt, liability or obligation of the Company or of any third party. No lender or other person dealing with the Company shall be concerned to see or inquire whether such prior consent is given.

VIII POWERS AND DUTIES OF MANAGEMENT COMMITTEE

38.The business of the Company shall be managed by the Management Committee, who may pay all expenses incurred in promoting and registering the Company, and may exercise all such powers of the Company, as are not, by the Act or by these Articles, required to be exercised by the Company in General Meeting, subject nevertheless to the provisions of the Act or the Articles and to such rules, being not inconsistent with the aforesaid provisions, as may be prescribed by the Company in accordance with Article 70 hereof or in General Meeting; but no rule made by the Company in General Meeting shall invalidate any prior act of the Management Committee which would have been valid if that regulation had not been made.

39.All cheques, promissory notes, drafts, bills of exchange and other negotiable instruments, and all receipts for moneys paid to the Company, shall be signed, drawn, accepted, endorsed, or otherwise executed, as the case may be, in such manner as the Management Committee shall from time to time by resolution determine

PROVIDED that all cheques shall be signed by not less than two members of the Management Committee.

40. The Management Committee shall cause minutes to be made in books provided for the purpose:

(i) of appointments of all officers of the Management Committee;
(ii) of the names of the Members of the Management Committee present at each meeting of the Management Committee and of any subcommittee of the Management Committee;
(iii) of all resolutions and proceedings at all meetings of the Company, and of the Management Committee, and of sub-committees of the Management Committee; and every Member of the Management Committee present at any meeting of the Management Committee or subcommittee of the Management Committee shall sign her/his name in a book to be kept for that purpose.

41. The Members of the Management Committee on behalf of the Company may make all reasonable and necessary provision for the payment of pensions and superannuation benefits to or in respect of employees and their dependants.

IX ADVISERS AND OBSERVERS

42. In managing the business of the Company pursuant to Article 38, the Management Committee shall have full power to seek and defray the cost of obtaining advice, including power to invite advisers and/or observers to attend and speak at its meetings (but not vote) on any issue before it for decision when professional expertise, including advice on the equal opportunities issues referred to in Part XX of these Articles, is required.

X DISQUALIFICATION OF MEMBERS OF THE MANAGEMENT COMMITTEE

43. The office of Member of the Management Committee shall be vacated if the said Member:

(i) holds any office of profit under the Company; or
(ii) becomes bankrupt or makes any arrangement or composition with her/his creditors generally; or
(iii) becomes prohibited from being such Member by reason of any order made under Section 295 of the Act; or
(iv) becomes of unsound mind; or
(v) resigns his/her office by notice in writing to the Company; or
(vi) is directly or indirectly interested in any contract with the Company (not being a contract or arrangement with another body established for charitable purposes only in which s/he is interested only as an unpaid director trustee or other officer of that other body) and fails to declare the nature of her/his interest in manner required by Section 317 of the Act.

44. A Member of the Management Committee shall not vote in respect of any contract in which s/he is interested or any matter arising out of any such contract and if s/he does so her/his vote shall not be counted.

XI APPOINTMENT AND REMOVAL OF MEMBERS OF MANAGMENT

COMMITTEE

45. The Company shall not be subject to Section 293 of the Act.

46.(a) The Company may by Ordinary Resolution at any time and from time to time appoint or remove a Member of the Management Committee.

(b) A Member of the Management Committee who falls without good reason to attend three consecutive meetings of the Management Committee shall automatically cease to be a Member of the Management Committee unless the Committee has previously (in its absolute discretion) decided otherwise.

(c) A Member of the Management Committee may be removed from office at any time by a two-thirds majority of the Committee present and voting at any meeting called for that purpose. Such Member shall have the right to appeal against his/her removal from office under this Article by giving notice of such to the Company Secretary at the registered office of the Company not less than seven days from the date of such meeting and the Company Secretary shall within five days of the receipt of such notice issue notice calling an Extraordinary General Meeting of the Company to be held on a date to be determined in consultation with the Officers elected pursuant to Article 55 hereof to review the decision of the Management Committee and decide whether to confirm it or re-instate the Member.

The Member concerned shall have the right to receive the same notice of the Extraordinary General Meeting as members of the Company and the right to speak in person (but not through any representative or adviser) at the Extraordinary General Meeting or to submit written representations to it but this shall not oblige the Company to adjourn its proceedings to facilitate the attendance of such Member or the drafting of any written representations.

(d) Pending the decision of the Extraordinary General Meeting of the Company the Member of the Management Committee concerned shall not be entitled to attend meetings of the Committee and, in the event of his/her reinstatement, no proceedings of the Management Committee shall be called into question by reason of their having been decided, undertaken or performed while such appeal is pending.

XII PROCEEDINGS OF MANAGEMENT COMMITTEE

47. The Management Committee may meet together for the despatch of business, adjourn and otherwise regulate its meetings as it thinks fit, and may determine the quorum necessary for the transaction of business provided always that the quorum shall not be less than three. It shall not be necessary to give notice of a meeting of the Management Committee to any Member thereof for the time being absent from the United Kingdom. A Member of the Management Committee may, and the Company Secretary on the requisition of any such Member shall, at any time summon a meeting of the Management Committee.

48. Questions arising at any meeting shall be decided by a majority of votes, and in the case of an equality of votes the Chair shall have a second or casting vote.

49. The continuing Members of the Management Committee may act notwithstanding any vacancy in their body, but, if and so long as their number is reduced below the number fixed by or pursuant to the articles of the Company is the necessary quorum of the Management Committee, the continuing Members or Member thereof may act for the purpose of increasing the number of Members to that number, or of summoning a general meeting of the Company, but for no other purpose.

50. The Members of the Management Committee may delegate any of their powers, other than the power to borrow, to sub-committees consisting of such members of their body (being not less than three) as they think fit and any subcommittee so formed shall in the exercise of the powers so delegated conform to any regulations that may be imposed on it by the Management Committee and shall not expend funds of the Company otherwise than in accordance with a budget agreed by the Management Committee. All acts and proceedings of any such subcommittee shall be reported back to the Management Committee as soon as possible.

51. A sub-committee may elect a Chair of its meetings; if no such Chair is elected, or if at any meeting the Chair is not present within five minutes after the time appointed for holding the same, the members present may choose one of their number to be Chair of the meeting.

52. A subcommittee may meet and adjourn as it thinks proper subject to the quorum being a minimum of three. Questions arising at any meeting shall be determined by a majority of votes of the Members present. In the case of an equality of votes the Chair shall have a second or casting vote.

53. All acts done by any meeting of the Management Committee or of a sub-committee of the Management Committee, or by any person acting as a Member of the Management Committee, shall notwithstanding that it be afterwards discovered that there was some defect in the appointment of any such Member of the Management Committee or person acting as aforesaid, or that they or any of them were disqualified, be as valid as if every such person had been duly appointed and was qualified to be a Member of the Management Committee.

54. A Resolution in writing signed by all the Members of the Management Committee for the time being entitled to receive notice of a meeting of the Management Committee shall be as valid and effectual as if it had been passed at a meeting of the Management Committee duly convened and held. Such Resolution may consist of several documents in the like form each signed by one or more of the Members of the Management Committee.

XIII OFFICERS TO BE APPOINTED BY MANAGEMENT COMMITTEE

55. The Members of the Management Committee at its first meeting after each Annual General Meeting of the Company shall elect honorary officers being a Chair, a Vice-Chair, an Honorary Committee Secretary (notwithstanding Article 58 hereof) and an Honorary Treasurer. In the absence of the Chair, one of the other honorary officers shall preside at any meeting of the Committee in the order set out above and if no such officer is present the Committee shall elect one other of their number to preside at the meeting in question.

56. Subject to the provisions of the Act the Company Secretary shall be appointed by the Management Committee for such term, at such remuneration and upon such conditions as they may think fit; any Company Secretary so appointed may be removed by them provided that no member of the Management Committee shall be appointed to the paid position of Company Secretary.

57. A provision of the Act or these Articles requiring or authorising a thing to be done by or to a Member of the Management Committee and the Company Secretary shall not be satisfied by its being done by or to the same person acting both as a Member of the Management Committee and as, or in place of, the Company Secretary.

XIV THE SEAL

58. The Management Committee shall provide for the safe custody of the Seal (if any) which shall only be used by the authority of the Management Committee or of a committee of the Management Committee authorised by the Management Committee in that behalf, and every instrument to which the Seal shall be affixed shall be signed by a Member of the Management Committee and shall be countersigned by the Company Secretary or by a second Member of the Management Committee or by some other person appointed by the Management Committee for the purpose.

XV   ACCOUNTS AND FINANCES

59. The Management Committee shall cause accounting records to be kept in accordance with Sections 221 to 223 inclusive of the Act.

60. The accounting records shall be kept at the registered office of the Company, or subject to sub-sections (1) and (2) of Section 222 of the Act at such other place or places as the Management Committee think fit, and shall always be open to the inspection of the officers of the Company.

61. The Management Committee shall from time to time determine whether and to what extent and at what times and places and under what conditions or regulations the accounts and books of the Company or any of them shall be open to the inspection of Members not being Members of the Management Committee, and no Member (not being a Member of the Management Committee) shall have any right of inspecting any account or book or document of the Company except as conferred by the Company

in General Meeting.

62. Members of the Management Committee shall from time to time in accordance with Sections 227, 229, 235, 236, 239, 241 and 242 of the Act cause to be prepared and to be laid before the Company in General Meeting such profit and loss accounts, balance sheets, group accounts (if any) and reports as are referred to in those Sections.

63. A copy of every balance sheet (including every document required by law to be annexed thereto) which is to be laid before the Company in General Meeting, together with a copy of the Auditor's report and Management Committee's report shall not less than twenty-one days before the date of the meeting be sent to every Member of, and every holder of debentures of, the Company Provided that this article shall not require a copy of these documents to be sent to any person of whose address the Company is not aware or to more than one of the joint holders of any debentures.

XVI AUDIT

64. Auditors shall be appointed and their duties regulated in accordance with Sections 236,237,247,252,253,262 and 384 to 392 inclusive and Part I of Schedule 8 of the Act.

XVII NOTICES

65. A notice may be given by the Company to any Member either personally or by sending it by post to her/him or to her/his registered address, or (if s/he has no registered address within the United Kingdom) to the address, if any, within the United Kingdom supplied by her/him to the Company for the giving of notice to her/him. Where a notice is sent by post, service of the notice shall be deemed to be effected by properly addressing, prepaying and posting a letter containing the notice, and to have been effected in the case of a notice of a meeting at the expiration of 24 hours after the letter containing the same is posted, and in any other case at the time at which the letter would be delivered in the ordinary course of post.

66. Notice of every General Meeting shall be given in any manner hereinbefore authorised to:

(i) every Member except those Members who (having no registered address within the United Kingdom) have not supplied to the Company an address within the United Kingdom for the giving of notices to them;
(ii) every person being a legal personal representative or a trustee in bankruptcy of a Member (having given to the Company notice of her/his appointment and an address in the United Kingdom for the service of notices) where the Member but for her/his death or bankruptcy would be entitled to receive notice of the meeting;
(iii) the Auditor for the time being of the Company;
(iv) any patron or patrons of the Company appointed pursuant to Article 72 hereof.

No other person shall be entitled to receive notices of General Meetings

XVIII   INDEMNIFY

67. In the execution of her/his duties and the exercise of her/his rights in relation to the affairs of the Company (and without prejudice to any indemnity to which s/he may otherwise be entitled) every Member of the Management Committee shall be entitled to be indemnified out of the assets of the Company against any costs, losses, claims, actions or other liabilities suffered or incurred by her/him and arising by reason of any improper investment made by or for the Company in good faith (so long as s/he shall have sought professional advice before making or procuring the making of suchinvestment) or by reason of any negligence or fraud of any agent engaged or employed by her/him in good faith (provided reasonable supervision shall have been exercised) notwithstanding the fact that the engagement or employment of such agent was strictly not necessary or by reason of any mistake or omission made in good faith by her/him or by reason of any other matter or thing other than deliberate fraud, wrongdoing or wrongful omission on the part of the Member of the Management Committee who is sought to be made liable. This clause shall only have effect insofar as it is not avoided by any provision of the Act.

XIX DISSOLUTION

68. The provisions of Clause 7 of the Memorandum of Association relating to the winding up or dissolution of the Company shall have effect as if the same were repeated in these Articles.

XX EQUAL OPPORTUNITIES

69.(a) Applications for membership of the Company shall be welcome from any individuals regardless of any issues concerned with race, creed, religion, culture, ethnic origin, sex or sexual orientation, marital status, any kind of disability or chronic illness, age and class, and the Company shall not be entitled to withhold or reject membership on the grounds of any such issue.

(b) The Management Committee, in managing the business of the Company, shall have regard to the equal opportunities implications of the issues under their deliberation and in particular the extent to which equal opportunities might be furthered by their decisions but, for the avoidance of doubt, shall not be bound to treat equal opportunities as the overriding consideration.

XXI   RULES OR BYE LAWS

70.(a) The Management Committee may from time to time make such Rules or Bye Laws as it may deem necessary or convenient for the proper conduct and management of the Company and for the purpose of prescribing classes of and conditions of membership, and in particular but without prejudice to the generality of the foregoing, it may by such Rules or Bye Laws regulate:

(i) The admission and classification of members of the Company, and the rights and privileges of such Members, and the conditions of membership and the terms on which Members may resign or have their membership terminated and the entrance fees, subscriptions and other fees or payments to be made by members.

(ii) The conduct of members of the Company in relation to one another, and to the Company's employees.

(iii) The setting aside of the whole or any part or parts of the Company's premises at any particular time or times or for any particular purpose or purposes.

(iv)The rights, privileges and obligations contained in any leases or property agreements issued to members in relation to property owned by the company and in relation to such other property occupied by other members of the Company.

(v) The procedure at General Meetings and meetings of the Committee and sub-committees in so far as such procedure is not regulated by these Articles.

(vl) And, generally, all such matters as are commonly the subjectmatter of Company rules.

(b) The Company in General Meeting shall have the power to alter or repeal the Rules or Bye Laws and to make additions to them and the Committee shall adopt such means as they deem sufficient to bring to the notice of members of the Company all such Rules or Bye Laws, which, so long as they shall be in force, shall be binding on all members of the Company Provided nevertheless that no Rule or Bye Law shall be inconsistent with, or shall affect or repeal anything contained in, the Memorandum or Articles of Association of the Company.

Signature Full name and Address

Dated   :
Witness :
Signature   :
Address :
Occupation   :

Model Rules for housing co-operatives provide a similar legal basis for the body's objectives and powers of operation as do the memorandum and articles for a limited company. This set of Model Rules is based upon the formal set of Rules registered with the Registrar of Friendly Societies by the Catalyst Collective Ltd., who assist in the registration of new co-operative bodies. It is the first set of Rules designed for a CoHousing Co-operative, and includes opportunity for the Co-operative to provide property for sale or rent.

Example 'Model Rules' for the registration of a "CoHousing Co-operative"

NAME AND STATUS

1a) The name of the society shall be ....CoHousing Co-operative Limited (referred to in these Rules as the Co-operative).

b) The Co-operative shall be a bona fide Co-operative within the meaning of section 1 (2) of the Industrial and Provident Societies Act 1965 and by virtue of its registration under that Act the liability of its members shall be limited to the extent of their shareholding.

OBJECTS

2 The objects of the Co-operative shall be as provided below. In carrying out these objects the Co-operative shall work towards the elimination of discrimination based on race, ethnic origin, nationality, gender, disability, sexuality, age, class, appearance, religion, responsibility for dependants, unrelated criminal convictions, a person's HIV antibody status or any other matter which causes any person to be treated with injustice.

a) The provision, construction, conversion, improvement, or management, on the Co-operative Principles, of accommodation exclusively for letting to members of the Co-operative under the terms of a tenancy or lease which

i) if a tenancy, shall be granted to them by the Co-operative and shall exclude all right for the members to assign the tenancy to any person other than the Co-operative (or a member of the Co-operative) and shall require the members to surrender or assign the tenancy to the Co-operative (or a member of the Co-operative) on their ceasing to be members, or
ii) if a lease, shall provide that each lessee, whether individual or joint, shall apply for membership of the Co-operative and, if accepted, remain a member until they give up the Lease; and that any lessee who ceases to be a member for any reason must, as soon as reasonably possible, assign the

lease to the Co-operative
[or a member of the Co-operative].
b) The provision and improvement, on the Co-operative Principles, of land, buildings, amenities, or services for the benefit of the members, either exclusively or in conjunction with other persons.

c) The provision of accommodation management services to members of the Co-operative and to the occupants of accommodation that is the subject of a management agreement under which the Co-operative is acting as managing agent for a landlord body.

d) The promotion of a combined private and communal life for and by all members of the Co-operative, based upon specific principles of CoHousing communities, whereby:
(i) the design of Co-operative accommodation is within 'intentional neighbourhoods' , such that the physical layout of the Co-operative's neighbourhood makes deliberate use of architectural and design features to maximise opportunities for intentional and incidental social contact;
(ii) all the accommodation within the 'neighbourhood' noted above is provided to the Co-operative's members as self-contained accommodation, supplemented by the availability of other shared and common local facilities, the extent and design of which the Co-operative's members will decide.

POWERS

3 The Co-operative shall have the power to do all things necessary or expedient for the fulfilment of its objects and for the support and development of bodies which are concerned with the provision and management of Co-operative accommodation or with the promotion of Co-operatives, or which have objects supported by the Co-operative. If the Co-operative is or, becomes a registered Housing Association under section 5 of the Housing Associations Act 1985, its powers under this rule shall be limited so as to conform to the requirements of the said Act.

TRADING

4 The Co-operative shall not trade for profit.

REGISTERED OFFICE

5 The registered office of the Co-operative shall be at ....
The office may be changed by resolution of a general meeting. Notice of any change shall be sent to the Registrar of Friendly Societies within fourteen days of such change or within such other time as may be required by the Treasury Regulations and in the manner and the form thereby prescribed.

SHARE CAPITAL

6 a) The share capital of the Co-operative shall consist of shares of the nominal value of £1 each issued to members of the Co-operative upon admission to membership.

b) Shares shall be neither withdrawable nor transferable, shall carry no right to interest, dividend or bonus, and shall be forfeited and cancelled upon cessation of membership from whatever cause and the amount paid up thereon shall become the property of the Co-operative.

MEMBERSHIP

7a) The members of the Co-operative shall be those persons signing the application for registration of the Co-operative and those persons whose names are entered in the register of members.

b) The register of members shall include the address of each member; it shall be the responsibility of the member to advise the Co-operative of any change. Any requirement in the Act or in the Rules of the Co-operative that a notice be served on the member shall be satisfied if notice has been delivered to the address given in the register.

c) Only persons aged 18 or over are eligible to become members.

d) All tenants of the Co-operative must be members and all members must be tenants or prospective tenants of the Co-operative.

e) A member shall hold only one share in the Co-operative. A maximum of two shares may be allocated to the combined holders of a joint-tenancy from the Co-operative, if the Co-operative has passed a Resolution to the effect that only two shares will be granted to a joint-tenancy, regardless of the number of joint-tenants. In the absence of passing such a Resolution all tenants within a joint-tenancy will each receive one share in the Co-operative.

8 Any application for membership shall be considered under the procedure laid down from time to time by general meeting. If an application is approved, the Co-operative will issue the applicant with one share upon payment of £1.

9 A member shall cease to be a member if:
a) they die; or
b) they resign either by writing to the Secretary or in person by a general meeting; or
c) they are expelled from membership by a general meeting; or
d) They cease to occupy the accommodation provided or managed by the Co-operative for a period of six months or their tenancy or lease is terminated. They shall cease to be members 28 days later, unless by that time they have either entered into a new tenancy or lease with the Co-operative or have been accepted as a prospective tenant; or
e) they are prospective tenants and have either
i) notified the Co-operative that they no longer require accommodation, or
ii) failed to respond in writing within 28 days to a written request, sent to their address in the register of members, to confirm that they still require accommodation.
iii) entered into a long leasehold agreement with the landlord of the property managed by, but not owned by, the Co-operative.

10 a) A member may be expelled by a resolution carried by the votes of three-quarters of the members present and voting at a Special General Meeting of the Co-operative of which notice has been duly given, provided that a complaint, in writing, of conduct detrimental to the interests of the Co-operative has been sent to them by order of the Co-operative. not less

than 28 days before the meeting. Such complaint shall contain particulars of the conduct complained of and shall call upon the member to answer the complaint and attend the meeting. At the meeting the members shall consider the evidence in support of the complaint and such evidence as the member may wish to place before them. If on due notice the member fails to attend the meeting, the meeting may proceed in their absence.

b) No person who has been expelled from membership shall be readmitted except by a resolution carried by the votes of at least three?quarters of the members present and voting at a Special General Meeting of which due notice has been given.

11a) A member may, in accordance with the Act, nominate a person or persons to whom any of their property held by the Co-operative, other than share capital, shall be transferred at their death.

b) Upon a claim being made to any property held by the Co-operative by the personal representatives of a deceased member pr the trustees in bankruptcy of a bankrupt member, the Co-operative shall pay or transfer any property to which the representative or trustee has become entitled.

GENERAL MEETINGS

12a) General meetings of the Co-operative may be attended by any member, and all members present shall be entitled to speak and vote. Each member shall personally be given at least seven clear days' notice of the time and place of each general meeting, and of the issues upon which decisions are to be taken. The Secretary shall call a general meeting as required by the Co-operative's rules or policies or decisions or at the written request of not less than three members or one?tenth of the members of the Co-operative, whichever is the greater, who may proceed to call the meeting if the Secretary does not do so within fourteen days of receipt of the request.

b) Special General Meetings of the Co-operative shall be conducted in the same manner as general meetings, except that they shall require twenty-eight clear days' notice to be given.

c) Each general meeting shall elect a chairperson whose function will be to conduct the business of the meeting in an orderly manner. The chairperson shall not have a casting vote; he or she shall have one vote as with any other member.

QUORUM

13 No business shall be transacted at any general meeting unless one?third of the Co-operative's members or 25 of them, whichever is the less, are present to start the meeting. If no quorum is present within half an hour of the time appointed for the meeting, the meeting shall stand adjourned. It shall be reconvened on the same day in the next week at the same time and place, (or such other time and place, as shall be agreed at the meeting) and notified to the members; and if at the reconvened meeting a quorum is not present within half an hour of the time appointed for the meeting the members present shall be a quorum.

VOTING

14 a) Decisions at a general meeting will be made on the principle of con-sensus agreement wherever possible. Where this does not prove possible then voting may take place as provided by Rule 14b.

b) Every member present in person at a general meeting shall have one vote, except where a Resolution has been passed under 7(e) above that has allocated two shares in the Co-operative to joint-tenancies, in which case each joint-tenancy will have the equivalent of two votes . Where only one member of a joint-tenancy is present, that member shall have one full vote at that General Meeting, and where two or more than two members of a joint tenancy are present the votes shall be split proportionately between those members. Except where otherwise specified in these Rules, resolutions shall be decided upon a majority vote of members present and voting. Votes shall be taken openly unless, before a motion is put to the vote, a secret ballot is demanded by not less than one tenth of the members present. Voting shall be conducted under the direction of the chairperson in accordance with any procedures agreed by the Co-operative.
A motion on which voting is tied shall be deemed to have fallen.

ANNUAL GENERAL MEETING

15 The Annual General Meeting shall be held within three months of the close of the financial year of the Co-operative. This meeting shall be called in the same manner as any Special General Meeting. It shall:
a) consider the frequency of general meetings during the coming year;
b) consider an annual report on the business of the Co-operative during the previous financial year;
c) receive the accounts and balance sheet for the previous financial year;
d) appoint an auditor if necessary according to Rule 36;
e) until such time as a Committee is elected following a resolution under Rule 17,
i) elect a Treasurer under the members' direction.
ii) elect a Secretary under the members' direction.

MANAGEMENT BY GENERAL MEETING

16 Until such time as a Committee is elected following a resolution under Rule 17:
a) the management of the Co-operative shall be undertaken by general meetings (at least one in every three months).

b) a general meeting shall constitute the committee of management and have power to make decisions in accordance with the Rules of the Co-operative.

c) a general meeting shall have the power to appoint, replace, and remove individuals, members, or groups of members delegated to exercise certain powers on behalf of the Co-operative.

d) a special general meeting shall have the power to adopt and issue Standing Orders to govern the terms and procedures for how the Co-operative operates, and for the terms and procedures that will govern how tenancies and leases with Co-operative members are to be issued and/or reviewed.

MANAGEMENT BY COMMITTEE

17a) A Committee to manage the Co-operative may be set up by a resolution carried by the votes of two?thirds of the members present and voting at a general meeting. The resolution shall take effect at the next Annual General Meeting unless the resolution specifies that it shall take effect at a Special General Meeting to be held before the next Annual General Meeting in accordance with Rule 17b. Except as provided for in Rule 17b, the elections to the Committee shall be declared at Annual General Meetings and elected Committee members shall enter upon their duties at the conclusion of the Annual General Meeting at which their election is declared.

b) If a Special General Meeting is required by a resolution passed under Rule 17a, the election of the Committee shall take place in accordance with Rules 19 and 20 except that references to the Annual General Meeting in those rules shall apply to the Special General Meeting at which the results of the election shall be declared and at the conclusion of which the Committee members shall enter upon their duties.

c) Subject to Rule 17b, until such time as a Committee is elected Rules 18 to 29 shall not apply.

POWERS OF COMMITTEE

18 a) The Committee shall have the power to do everything necessary to manage the Co-operative except to determine issues specifically designated under these Rules as a responsibility of a general meeting.

b) The general meeting shall retain responsibility for the adoption of regulations and procedures governing the election and composition of the Committee and the term of office of Committee members. The general meeting may adopt a resolution delegating some or all of this responsibility to the Committee, and may revoke such delegation.

c) The Committee shall report on the affairs of the Co-operative to each general meeting and shall submit an annual report to the Annual General meeting.

NOMINATIONS FOR COMMITTEE

19 a) Only members of the Co-operative are eligible to be nominated for election to the Committee.

b) Nomination of candidates for election to the Committee may be accepted at the Annual General Meeting unless a general meeting has passed a resolution requiring nominations to be in writing and signed by the member nominated and handed to the Secretary or delivered to the registered office of the Co-operative a specified number of days, not being less than three nor more than fourteen, before the date appointed for the Annual General Meeting.

ELECTION OF COMMITTEE

20 a) If the number of nominees does not exceed the number of Committee members to be elected, then each nominee shall be elected by a simple majority vote of members.

b) If the number of nominees exceeds the number of Committee members to be elected, then the members to serve on the Committee shall be elected from amongst them by ballot. Unless previously delegated to the Committee under Rule 18b, a general meeting shall make regulations governing the conduct of the ballot, provided that each member shall be entitled to one vote for each vacancy to be filled but shall not give more than one vote to any one candidate.

REMOVAL OF COMMITTEE MEMBERS

21 A general meeting may remove any one or more of the Committee members by a resolution carried by a simple majority of the members present and voting provided that at least seven clear days notice of the motion has been given to all members of the Co-operative. The general meeting may proceed to fill any vacancy thus caused.

VACANCIES ON COMMITTEE

22 a) Except for Committee members co?opted under Rule 24, any Committee member who ceases to be a member of the Co-operative shall immediately cease to be a member of the Committee.

b) Except as provided by Rules 20 and 21, any vacancy caused by the death, resignation, retirement or removal of any Committee member may be filled by the Committee.

SIZE AND QUORUM OF COMMITTEE

23 The Committee shall consist of not less than seven or more than fifteen members as determined by a general meeting, The quorum of the Committee shall be one?third of the number determined as its membership, unless a general meeting sets a higher quorum.

CO-OPTIONS TO COMMITTEE

24 The Committee may co?opt any persons to serve as Committee members, subject to any limitation made by a general meeting and providing that there shall always be a majority of elected Committee members on the Committee. Co?opted Committee members may be removed by resolution of the Committee or by general meeting under Rule 21.

SUBCOMMITEE

25 The Committee may establish subcommittees consisting of at least one Committee member and other persons as the Committee shall think fit, provided that a majority of any subcommittee shall be members of the Co-operative. The powers and proceedings of a subcommittee shall be determined by the Committee in written terms of reference.

ELECTION OF CHAIRPERSON BY COMMITTEE

26 The Committee shall, at its first meeting after the Annual General Meeting of the Co-operative, elect a chairperson from amongst its number to hold office until the first Committee meeting after the following Annual General Meeting unless removed or replaced by the Committee.

ELECTION OF SECRETARY AND TREASURER

27 The Committee shall elect a Secretary and a Treasurer who shall serve under its direction until removed or replaced by the Committee.

PROCEEDINGS OF COMMITTEE

28 Except where provided otherwise in these Rules, the Committee shall determine issues by a majority of Committee members present and voting. If any vote is tied, the proposal shall be deemed to have fallen. The chairperson shall normally preside at Committee meetings. If at any Committee meeting the chairperson is absent or declines to act, the Committee shall elect one of its number to chair the meeting.

DECLARATION OF COMMITTEE MEMBERS' INTERESTS

29 If a member of the Committee has an interest in a matter under discussion by the Committee they shall disclose the nature of the interest to the Committee and may be required by any Committee member to be absent from the meeting while the matter is determined.

OFFICERS

30 The Co-operative's officers shall be the Secretary and Treasurer, and such others as may be appointed from time to time. The officers shall discharge their powers and responsibilities in accordance with these Rules. and with such regulations, standing orders, policies, and procedures as may be established by the Co-operative consistently with these Rules.

a) The Secretary shall ensure that meetings are properly called and minutes kept, that the register of members and officers is maintained, that the use of the seal is recorded, and that the appropriate returns are made to the Registrar of Friendly Societies.

b) The Treasurer shall manage the financial affairs of the Co-operative and ensure that adequate records are kept.

PAYMENTS TO OFFICERS AND COMMITTEE

31 The Co-operative shall not remunerate any member of the Co-operative or any member of any Committee established by the Co-operative in respect of service as a member of any such Committee or as an officer or member. This Rule shall not prevent the reimbursement of expenses properly incurred by any person on behalf of the Co-operative.

BORROWING POWERS

32 a) The Co-operative shall have power to borrow money, including the issue of loan stock, for the purposes of the Co-operative provided that, at the time of borrowing, the sum of the amount remaining undischarged of monies borrowed and the amount of the proposed borrowing shall not exceed £10 million and that for this purpose:

i) the amount remaining undischarged of any index?linked monies previously borrowed by the Co-operative or on any deep discounted security shall be deemed to be the amount required to repay such borrowing in full if such borrowing became repayable at the time of the proposed borrowing, and

ii) the amount of any proposed borrowing intended to be index?linked or on any deep discounted security shall be deemed to be the proceeds of such proposed borrowing receivable by the Co-operative at the time of the proposed borrowing.

b) In the case of any loan, the Co-operative shall not pay interest at a rate exceeding that necessary to obtain and retain sufficient capital to carry out the Co-operative's objects.

c) The Co-operative shall have the power to determine from time to time the terms and conditions upon which money is borrowed or loan stock issued and to vary such terms and conditions subject to the provisions of this Rule.

d) The Co-operative shall have the power to mortgage or charge any of its property, to issue debentures and other securities, and to charge any or all of its assets as security for money borrowed.

e) The Co-operative shall not receive money on deposit.

f) The Co-operative may receive from any source donations towards the work of the Co-operative.

g) The Co-operative shall have the power to guarantee a loan to any corporate society registered under the Act, or any company registered under the Companies Acts, whose rules are drawn on the Co-operative principles and include clauses preventing the distribution of increased equity value of their land, buildings or equipment to their individual members, past or present, either upon the withdrawal of members from a membership, or arising from the sale or transfer of property by the society or company upon dissolution or otherwise and such other principles as a general meeting shall approve from time to time.

If necessary, the Co-operative shall have the power to mortgage or charge any of its property to secure such a guarantee.

INVESTMENT

33 a) The funds of the Co-operative may, to the extent permitted by the law for the time being in force, be invested:

i) in any manner expressly authorised by the Act:

ii) in any investments covered by Parts I, II and III of the First Schedule to the Trustee Investments Act 1961 or in stocks and shares or debentures of any body corporate but subject in the case of any investments under paragraphs 1 and 3 of Part III or of any body incorporated overseas to the taking of advice in accordance with the provisions of section 6 of the Trustee Investments Act 1961:

iii) in shares or on security of any Industrial and Provident Society:

iv) in any freehold, feuhold, or leasehold property whatever in the United Kingdom:

but shall not be invested otherwise.

b) The Co-operative may, to the extent permitted by the law for the time being in force, engage the services of a suitable person to assist in the exercise of the management or investment of the property for the time being forming part of the property of the Co-operative. A suitable person shall be a person whom the Co-operative reasonably believes to be qualified by ability and experience in the matters delegated, and who is an authorised or exempted person for the purposes of Part I of the Financial Services Act 1986 as amended or re-enacted from time to time.

c) The Co-operative may appoint any member or members to vote on its behalf at meetings of any other body corporate in which the Co-operative has invested any part of its funds.

PAYMENTS TO MEMBERS

34 No portion of the income or the property of the Co-operative shall be transferred either directly or indirectly by way of dividend, bonus or otherwise by way of profit to members of the Co-operative except insofar as the tenancy or lease may provide upon surrender to the Co-operative for payments to be made to the member.

SURPLUSES

35a) The Co-operative may apply any surpluses towards carrying out the objects of the Co-operative.

b) A general meeting may set aside any part of the surpluses arising in any year to be donated or loaned for any purposes determined by the members in general meeting, provided such purposes are in accordance with the objects of the Co-operative.

c) Any surpluses not applied or set aside shall be carried forward.

AUDIT AND ANNUAL RETURNS

36 a) Subject to any statutory exemptions or regulations as may be in force, the Co-operative shall in accordance with sections 4 and 8 of the Friendly and Industrial and Provident Societies Act 1968 appoint in each year one or more auditors to whom the accounts of the Co-operative for that year shall be submitted for audit as required by the said Act and shall have all such rights in relation to notice of and audience at general meetings, access to books and the supply of information, and otherwise as are provided by the said Act. Every such auditor shall be appointed by the Co-operative at a general meeting, and in the case of any auditor so appointed who is a qualified auditor under section 7 of the said Act, the provisions of sections 5 and 6 thereof apply to the reappointment, removal or replacement of the said auditor.

b) Every year not later than the date provided by the Act or where the return is made up to the date allowed by the Registrar not later than three months after such date the Secretary shall send the Registrar of Friendly Societies in the form prescribed the Co-operative's annual return relating to its affairs for the period required by the Act together with auditors' reports and/or balance sheets as required by the Act or other relevant statutes.

MINUTES, RECORDS AND SEAL

37a) Sufficient records shall be maintained and left at the registered office for the purposes of the Co-operative and to comply with the provisions of the Act.

b) The Co-operative shall have a seal kept in the custody of the Secretary and used only by the authority of the Co-operative. Sealing shall be attested by the signatures of the Secretary and two members of the Co-operative.

DISPUTES

38a) Provided that any internal disputes procedure established by the Co-operative has been exhausted, any dispute concerning matters governed by these Rules between a member, or any person aggrieved who has not for more than six months ceased to be a member, and the Co-operative or an officer thereof, may at the request of either party be submitted to an arbitrator appointed by mutual agreement of both parties whose decision shall be binding and conclusive, and application for the enforcement thereof may be made by either party to the County Court.

b) The costs of arbitration shall be born as the arbitrator directs, and the complaining party shall before arbitration deposit with the Co-operative's solicitor the sum of £50 which shall be refunded provided that the complaining party complies with the decision reached by the arbitration.

AMENDMENT OF RULES

39 Any Rule herein may be rescinded or amended or a new Rule made by resolution of three?quarters of the members present and voting at a Special General Meeting, providing that all members of the Co-operative have been supplied with copies of the proposed amendment at least seven days before the meeting at which it is to be determined. No amendment of these Rules is valid until registered by the Registrar of Friendly Societies.

TRANSFER OF ENGAGEMENTS: DISSOLUTION

40 a) A general meeting may agree to accept a transfer of engagements from any Industrial and Provident Society having objects consistent with those of the Co-operative.

b) A Special General Meeting may agree by a resolution supported by three-quarters of the members present and voting to transfer the Co-operative's engagements to any Industrial and Provident Society whose objects include providing accommodation.

c) The Co-operative may be dissolved by the consent of three?quarters of the members by their signatures to an instrument of dissolution provided for in the Treasury Regulations or by winding up in the manner provided for in the Act.
d) Any surpluses remaining after settlement of the Co-operative's debts and liabilities should be donated or transferred to any Industrial and Provident Society whose objects include providing accommodation.

INTERPRETATION

41 In these Rules, unless the subject matter or context are inconsistent therewith:

a) words importing the singular or plural shall include the plural or singular respectively;

b) "the Act" refers to the Industrial and Provident Societies Acts 1965 to 1978, or any Act or Acts amending or in substitution for them for the time being in force;

c) "the Co-operative Principles" refers to the most up?to?date principles adopted by the International Co-operative Alliance and to the proposed "Principles of a Co-operative 'Intentional neighbourhood'" attached to this Rule;

d) "tenant" shall mean any person other than a body corporate who holds, either individually or jointly, a tenancy or lease entitling them to occupy residential property owned by the Co-operative;

e) "surpluses" shall mean any money remaining after the Co-operative's current expenditure and obligations have been provided for and adequate allowance has been made for the Co-operative's reasonably foreseeable future requirements;

f) "Treasury Regulations" shall mean regulations made in accordance with section 71 of the Industrial and Provident Societies Act 1965.

g) "clear days" in relation to the period of notice means the period excluding the day when the notice is given or deemed to be given and the day for which it is given or on which it is to take effect.

I

Name:

2.

Name:

3.

Name:

Secretary:
Name:

The new legislation to set up new 'Commonhold Associations' is to be brought into force on a date to be fixed by Government. This could not be before the Land Registration Act 2002 came into force on 13 October 2003. An announcement on the commencement of new regulations will be made in due course.

The procedure that is proposed for the formal establishment of a new 'commonhold' interest is that the 'commonhold association' must be incorporated before any application can be made to the Land Registry to denote a site as having a 'commonhold' character. The key stages of this process will be in the following order:

creation of the commonhold association;

application for registration of the land as a freehold estate in commonhold land; and

registration of the land as such.

Detail is provided on the basis for the creation of the new association, drawn from material produced by the Lord Chancellor's Department.

Registration as a Commonhold Association

'Commonhold' is to be a new form of land ownership in England and Wales, created by Part 1 of the Commonhold and Leasehold Reform Act 2002. It will combine freehold ownership of a unit in a larger development with membership of a commonhold association that owns and is responsible for the management and upkeep of the common parts of the development.

At present there are two forms of land tenure in England and Wales: freehold and leasehold. Commonhold will be a species of freehold ownership. It will provide a framework in which freehold ownership of a part of a multi-occupied development will be combined with the ability to enforce positive covenants against other owners. Previously, this has only been satisfactorily achievable in relation to interdependent properties by adopting a leasehold structure. By removing the legal barrier that the burden of a positive covenant does not bind a successor in title of the original covenantor, commonhold has been designed to reduce or obviate the need to create a lease and, therefore, to have a landlord. Commonhold is proposed to be an alternative to long leasehold ownership of flats and other interdependent properties.

The Act provides the general legal framework for the creation, running and termination of commonhold communities. The detail is to be set out in secondary legislation.

A Consultation Paper was issued by the Lord Chancellor's Department Consultation Paper - Commonhold Proposals for Commonhold Regulations, in October 2002. This paper set out for consultation provisional policy proposals to inform the drafting of the regulations to be made to implement Part I of the Commonhold and Leasehold Reform Act 2002. When made the regulations will govern the formation, running and termination of commonhold communities.

The purpose of the consultation was to canvass views on proposals for the matters to be included in the regulations to be made under the Act with particular reference to:
- the creation of a commonhold;
- the constitution of the commonhold association; and
- the rights and duties of the unit-holders and the com monhold association.

The initial impact assessment of the proposals as carried out by the Lord Chancellors Department indicates that commonhold should offer the following advantages over long leasehold ownership:
- the standardisation of documentation should
- assure quality, make the legal documentation more accessible and reduce the cost of advice;
- the ownership of a lease, which is a wasting asset, will be replaced by ownership of a freehold, which is not;
- the community will manage its own affairs without
- alternative dispute resolution procedures will be established to reduce recourse to the courts.

These advantages can be replicated in the best long leasehold developments but commonhold will offer a largely uniform product wherever it is found.

Commonholds will have to be created expressly by registration at the Land Registry. The essential preconditions for the creation of a commonhold are that a commonhold association has been created and that the applicant for registration of the commonhold is the registered proprietor of the freehold land to comprise the commonhold.

The application to the Land Registry for registration of the land as a freehold estate in commonhold land will have to be accompanied by three principal documents:
- The memorandum of association of
  the commonhold association;
- The articles of association of
  the commonhold association; and
- The commonhold community statement.

The form and content of all three will be prescribed in regulations. Together, these documents form the constitution of the commonhold, defining the mutual rights and duties of the unit-owners and the commonhold association. Inevitably, the quality of freehold ownership of a unit cannot be as unrestricted in an inter-dependent development as in an independent property. Setting the appropriate balance between the rights of the individual on the one hand and the rights of the community on the other is one of the main objectives of regulations.

The concept and much of the content of the specimen memorandum and articles of a commonhold association will be familiar to anyone dealing with companies and company law. The commonhold community statement is, however, a new creation. The commonhold community statement sets out the management framework and the rules of the commonhold including the rights and duties of the unit-holders and of the commonhold association. However, it is not entirely comprehensive and must be read in conjunction with the memorandum and articles of association and with the registers of the common parts and unit titles. In the event of any conflict between the memorandum and articles and the commonhold community statement, the provisions of the memorandum and articles will prevail.

The specimen draft commonhold community statement has four parts and begins as follows:

"COMMONHOLD COMMUNITY STATEMENT
[NAME] COMMONHOLD ASSOCIATION LTD

This Commonhold Community Statement (referred to as "this Statement") is to be read together with the memorandum and articles of association of the company referred to above (referred to in this Statement as the "Memorandum", the "Articles" and the "Commonhold Association" respectively). In the event of any conflict between the provisions of this Statement and the Memorandum and Articles, the provisions of the memorandum and articles shall prevail.

This Statement may only be amended in accordance with sections 23, 24, 30 and 33 of the Act and regulations made thereunder (as applicable).

FURTHER INFORMATION ABOUT THE COMMONHOLD [ENTER NAME OF COMMONHOLD] MAY BE FOUND IN THE MEMORANDUM AND ARTICLES OF ASSOCIATION OF THE [ ] COMMONHOLD ASSOCIATION AND BY LOOKING AT THE RELEVANT REGISTERS KEPT BY HM LAND REGISTRY."

The respective parts of the Community Statement will then cover the following issues:

Part I describes the commonhold organisation, the commonhold land and the applicant for registration.
Part II of the community statement describes the commonhold, i.e. a plan and description of the type of Commonhold, total number of units, (residential only, commercial only, or mixed use, etc) and will define the extent of each commonhold unit :

Part III of the community statement defines the rights of the developer during the development of the commonhold following the registration of the land as commonhold and culminating with the sale of the final unit.

Part IV sets out the rules of the commonhold association in eight sections, including the use of the commonhold; insurance; repair and maintenance; financial matters; dispute resolution and more general rules.

Part V of the community statement provides space for additional information to record special or unusual features of the individual commonhold.

Part VI provides for the signature of the community statement by the applicants for registration of the commonhold at the Land Registry.

Definition A CoHousing 'organisation' is taken to mean an autonomous association of households united in their aspirations to meet shared residential and social needs within a jointly?owned and democratically?controlled 'intentional neighbourhood'.

Values and Principles

CoHousing organisations are based on the values of social responsibility, democracy, equality, equity and solidarity, and on caring for others. CoHousing members will believe in the worth of a practical setting in which those values can be lived in practice. The following principles are guidelines by which CoHousing organisations can strive to put their values for 'intentional neighbourhoods' into practice:

1st Principle: Neighbourhood membership

CoHousing organisations are bodies which are open to all persons that come to live within the CoHousing neighbourhood and who are willing to accept the responsibilities of such neighbourhood membership.

2nd Principle: Control by a democracy of members

CoHousing organisations are bodies that are controlled by all their members, actively agreeing in daily policies and guidelines that focus upon the common neighbourhood life. All elected representatives are accountable to the membership as a whole. Households will have equal voting rights in the manner that the whole membership agrees.

3rd Principle: Members and their economic participation

All members contribute to the financial and social capital of their collective neighbourhood. At least part of that capital is usually the common property of the CoHousing body. It will be for the CoHousing body to decide the terms, if any, on which members might be able to receive a return on any capital directed towards living in the CoHousing neighbourhood as a condition of membership. Members allocate any resources from the CoHousing body in order to develop their organisation and neighbourhood; to maintain their common property and other facilities; and in other activities to support individual members in proportion to their transactions with the CoHousing body, as approved by the overall membership.

4th Principle: Autonomy and independence

CoHousing organisations are autonomous, self?help organisations controlled by their members. If they enter into agreements with other organisations, including local or state authorities, or raise capital from external sources, they do so on terms that reinforce their members' democratic control and maintain the collective autonomy of their CoHousing neighbourhood.

5th Principle: Education, training and information

CoHousing organisations provide education and training for all their members, and for any managers or employees, in order that they can all contribute effectively to the development of their neighbourhoods. CoHousing organisations may extend this education towards the external public to inform others about the nature and benefits of such shared 'intentional neighbourhoods'.

6th Principle: Co-operation among CoHousing neighbourhoods

CoHousing organisations serve their members most effectively and strengthen the CoHousing movement by working together through local, national, regional and international contacts and associated structures.

7th Principle: Concern for the neighbourhood community

CoHousing organisations work to sustain the development of their communities and neighbourhoods and the policies approved by their members will reflect how the one will support and strengthen the other.

[* This proposal acknowledges and is based upon the "International Co-operative Alliance - 'Statement on the Co-operative identity'".]

11 questions to put to a potential partner during 'interview'

(such as a Housing Association or a Housing Developer)

1. What is their understanding of the term 'CoHousing'?

2. Any experience of visiting a 'CoHousing' neighbourhood?
[And if 'Yes', what are the details...]

3. Any experience of working with a 'CoHousing' project or Group? [And if 'Yes', what are the details...]

4. What has been their experience of working with community groups?

5. Any experience of working with mixed-income initiatives? [And if 'Yes', what are the details...]

6. Have they involved prospective resident households into the development and management of a 'community housing' project? [And if 'Yes', what are the details]

7. Who has been involved in the previous work?

8. Who would be involved in this project, if appointed, and what has been their specific experience?

9. Will they be available for meetings at evenings or weekends, if required?

10. Has the organisation been a partner to a project where they were not the 'lead' partner, and would they have a concern about taking part on those terms, if that was the case?

11. What would be the basis of their fees, or the cost to the Group?

Select Bibliography and Contacts

Texts relevant to CoHousing development in the UK:

BRENTON M. (1998) 'We're in charge. 'CoHousing Communities of older people in the Netherlands: lessons for Britain,?. Bristol, Policy Press.

DIGGERS AND DREAMERS : The Guide to Communal Living, D & D Pub

FIELD M (2000) "Targets for Intentional Communities?" 'Axis', Aug/Sep. 2000 issue, and on DETR-sponsored website 'RegenNet'

HANSON C. (1996) The CoHousing Handbook, Hartley & Marks, Point Roberts, USA

THE HOCKERTON COMMUNITY (2001) The Sustainable Community - A Practical Guide. (Website : www.hockerton.demon.co.uk)

HOUSING FOR WOMEN / HOUSING CORPORATION (2002) "The Legal and Financial feasibility of setting up a CoHousing community for older women in London", Housing For Women, London

McCAMANT K & DURRETT C. (1988.rev1994) CoHousing. a contempo-rary approach to housing ourselves. Berkeley, California. Ten Speed Press.

NEAL P. ed. (2003) Urban Villages and the Making of Communities, Spon Press, London, UK

NELSON L. (1997) CoHousing : Designs for Living, Eco Design, Vol.V, No.2

ROGERS D. & FIELD M. (1998) 'Legal and financial frameworks for CoHousing projects', (in Brenton M. op cit.)

WATES N (2000) The Community Planning Handbook.. Earthscan,

Other texts:

BARTON H. et al (2000) Sustainable Communities, Earthscan, UK

BARTON H. & TSOUROU C (2000) Healthy Urban Planning, Spon Press (on behalf of World Health Organisation)

BIRCHALL J. (1988) Building Communities, the Co-operative Way, Routledge Kegan Paul, UK

BRENTON M. (1999) Choice, autonomy and mutual support: older women's collaborative living arrangements. York: York Publishing Services/Joseph Rowntree Foundation.
(2001) 'Older People's CoHousing Communities' in S.Peace & C.Holland (eds) Inclusive Housing for an Ageing Society'. Bristol, Policy Press.

BROWN T. et al (2000) Stakeholder Housing, Pluto Press, London

CDS Co-operatives, 'Model rules for housing co-operatives'. CDS, 3 Marshalsea Road, London SE1 IEP

CHANON G "Community Responses to Social Exclusion", in Policy Responses to Social Exclusion, Percy-Smith J. et al (2000), OUP

COATES C. (2001) Utopia Britannica, D & D Publications, London

DEPARTMENT OF THE ENVIRONMEN T, TRANSPORT & THE REGIONS Planning for Communities of the Future, London, HMSO, (1997) Sustainability Counts (1998)

A Better Quality of Life : the Government's National Sustainable Development Strategy, (1999)
By Design : Urban Design in the Planning System, (2000)
Local Quality of Life Counts (2000)
Millennium Villages and Sustainable Communities, (2000)
Our Towns and Cities : the future (Urban White Paper), (2000)
Prepare an Effective Local Agenda 21 Strategy , (2000)
Quality and Choice : a decent home for all (Green Paper), (2000)
Sustainable Development Research : Gaps and Opportunities, (2000)
Sustainable Local Communities for the 21st Century : Why and How to
Quality & choice for older people's housing: a strategic framework(2001)

DUFFY K. & HUTCHINSON J.(1997) "Urban policy and the turn to community" Town Planning Review, 68, 347-362

ENO S & TREANOR D (1982) The Collective Housing Handbook, Laurieston Hall Publications, Castle Douglas, Scotland

FAIRLIE S. (1996) Low Impact Development : Planning and People in a Sustainable Countryside, Jon Carpenter Publishing, Oxfords.

FIELD M (2001) "Policies to support the creation of new neighbourhood communities", Proceedings of the 'International Sustainable Development Research Conference - Manchester, 2001', ERP Environment, Shipley, UK (2001) "Obstacles to Creating New 'Neighbourhood Communities' in UK", Paper given to the "International Community Studies Association" in ZEGG, Berlin, June 2001

FICH M.et al(1995) Old People's Houses, Kunstakademiets Forlag, Cophag

FROMM D. (1991) Collaborative communities : CoHousing, central living and other forms of housing with shared facilities, Reinhold, New York

GEHL J. (1987) Life Between Buildings, Van Nostrand Reinhold, New York

GINSON T. (1996) The Power in Our Hands, Jon Carpenter, Charlbury,UK

GRAYSON L. (2000) The Housing Challenge : a review of the issues, The Planning Exchange, Glasgow

HALL P. (1996) Cities of Tomorrow, Blackwell, Oxford, UK

HALL P. & WARD C. (1998) Sociable Cities - the Legacy of Ebenezer Howard, Wiley, Chichester

HALPERN.D(2004) Social Capital, Polity Press.

HANDY C (1988) Understanding Voluntary Organisations - how to make them function effectively, Penguin ISBN 0-14-014338-6

HARDY D.(1979) Alternative Communities in Nineteenth Century England, Longman, New York
(2001)Utopian England: Community Experiments 1900-1945,Spon.London

HEALEY P. (1997) Collaborative Planning, Macmillan, Basingstoke, UK

HILDUR J .(Ed. 1999) Creating Harmony.: conflict resolution in community. Gaia Trust/Permanent pub. ISBN 1-85623-014-7

HOURIET R. (1973) Getting Back Together, Sphere Books, London, UK

HULL A. (1997) "Restructuring the debate on allocating land for housing growth", Housing Studies, Vol 12, No 3, p367-382

INSTITUTE FOR PUBLIC POLICY RESEARCH (2000), Housing United :Final Report of the Forum on the Future of Social Housing, IPPR London

LOCAL GOVERNMENT ASSOCIATION (2000), Vision into Reality : the future strategic housing role of local authorities, LGA, London

MARKHAM THORSONS U (1996) Managing Conflict : how to deal with difficult situations at work. Ursula. ISBN 0-7225-3109-5

METCALF B. (1998) "Sustainable communal living around the globe : Yesterday, Today and Tomorrow", paper presented at Creating Sustainable Community Conference, Findhorn, Oct/98

National Housing Federation, Model management agreements for the tenant management of housing owned by an RSL are available from the NHF, 175 Grays Inn Road, London WCIX 5UP.

NORWOOD K. & SMITH K. (1995) Rebuilding Community in America, Shared Living Resource Centre, University of California

ODPM (Office of the Deputy Prime Minister) (2002) Living Places : Cleaner, Safer, Greener, HMSO
(2003) Sustainable communities: building for the future, HMSO,

OSPINA J (1987) Housing Ourselves, Hilary Shipman, London

PEARSON L. (1988) The Architectural & Social History of Co-operative Living, Macmillan, Basingstoke, UK

PERCY-SMITHH J(2000)Policy Responses to Social Exclusion,OUPress UK

THE PRINCE'S FOUNDATION (2000) Sustainable Urban Extensions : Planned through Design, Prince's Foundation/English Partnerships, London

RIGBY A. (1974) Communes in Britain, Routledge Kegan Paul, London

ROOM (2000) Defining Positive Planning : briefing paper for consultation, National Council for Housing and Planning, London

ROSLIN M. & FIELD M. (1998) 'Mini-neighbourhoods', Resurgence, No.190

SCHWARZ W. & D. (1998) Living Lightly : Travels in Post-consumer Society, Jon Carpenter, Charlbury, UK

SOCIAL EXCLUSION UNIT (2001) A New Commitment to Neighbourhood Renewal : National Strategy Action Plan, London, HMSO

SOMERVILLE P. (1998) "Empowerment through residence", Housing Studies, Vol 13, No 2, p233-257

STOCKDALE A. & LLOYD G. (1998) "Forgotten Needs? The demographic and socio-economic impact of free-standing new settlements", Housing Studies, Vol 13, No 1, p43-58

STUTLEY R. (2001) The Definitive Business Plan, Prentice Hall, US

TURNER J (1976) Housing by People - Towards Autonomy in Building Environments, Marion Boyars, London

URBAN DESIGN GROUP Urban Design Source Book, UDG, London

URBAN TASK FORCE (1999) Towards an Urban Renaissance, London,

WARD C. (1990) Talking Houses, Freedom Press, London
(1996) Talking to Architects, Freedom Press, London

YOUNG M. & LEMOS G. (1997) The Communities We Have Lost and Can Regain, Lemos & Crane, London

ZAHLE K. & MORTENSEN P.D. (1992) "Collective and Co-operative Housing", Open House International, Vol.17, No.2, p56-65

Key Websites:

buildingforlife.org Building for Life is a commitment to the quality of new homes made by 3 key partners: the house-building industry, represented by the House Builders Federation ; government, represented by the Commission for Architecture & the Built Environment (CABE); and campaigners, represented by the Civic Trust

cch.coop Website of the Confederation of Co-operative Housing - the UK organisation for housing co-operatives, tenant-controlled housing organisations and regional federations of housing co-ops.

charity-commission.gov.uk Registrar of Charities website, main source of information on legal documents, charity structures.

cohousing.co.uk A window on the cohousing scene in the UK covering existing and forming groups. Carries ads for groups looking for new members and properties for sale in exisiting Cohousing schemes as well as various discussion papers.

cohousing.org The Cohousing Association of the United States (Coho/US) is an organization whose purpose is to promote and encourage the cohousing concept, support both individuals and groups in creating communities, provide assistance to completed groups for improving their systems for living together in community, and provide networking opportunities for those involved or interested in cohousing.

communitiestakingcontrol.org This site is about communities in England setting up community initiatives to tackle issues important to local communities. The site is primarily aimed at tenants of housing associations, but because it is about a wide range of community control opportunities, much of the information will be relevant to tenants and communities in general.

companieshouse.gov.uk Main registration authority for companies and source of public information.

ctegrants.org.uk Community Training & Enabling grants are designed to support housing association residents in England to develop new training and community development projects.

diggersanddreamers.org.uk If you're interested in joining or setting up some kind of intentional community then this is thewebsitefor you. you'll find news, views and other useful resources including a fully searchable database of communities in Britain.

fsa.gov.uk The Financial Services Agency aims to maintain efficient, orderly and clean financial markets and help retail consumers achieve a fair deal. It aims to help consumers become better informed about financial matters, for example with information on : endowment mortgages; advice on comparative mortgages; consumer help; resources for Teaching and Learning

hbf.co.uk The House Builders Federation (HBF) is the principal trade federation for private sector housebuilders and voice of the house building industry in England and Wales.

housingcorp.gov.uk The Homepage of the Housing Corporation,

that funds and regulates housing associations in England and Wales
jrf.org.uk The Joseph Rowntree Foundation is one of the largest social policy research and development charities in the UK. It spends about £7 million a year on a research and development programme that seeks to better understand the causes of social difficulties and explore ways of better overcoming them. It also engages in practical housing and care work through the Joseph Rowntree Housing Trust, and is currently involved in the planning of a new 540-home housing development in York.

lease-advice.org The Leasehold Advisory Service is an independent advice agency, funded by Government grant. It provides free advice to leaseholders, landlords, professional advisers and others on the law affecting residential leasehold property.

nihe.gov.uk Homepage of the Northern Ireland Housing executive, that funds and regulates housing associations in Northern Ireland.

princes-foundation.org The Prince's Foundation for the Built Environment is an educational charity established by The Prince of Wales to teach and demonstrate in practice those principles of traditional urban design and architecture which put people and the communities of which they are part at the centre of the design process. The website includes the detail of the new 'Urban Network' which has replaced the Urban Villages Forum.

regen.net Information network for mutli-agency partnerships involved in urban regeneration, rural regeneration, economic development and community development.

rtpi.org.uk The RTPI exists to advance the science and art of town planning for the benefit of the public.
It is a membership organisation, and a registered charity. Most of its members are fully qualified professional planners. Nearly two thirds work as planning officers for local councils. Others work for central government, for property developers and other organisations with significant landholdings, as consultants or as teachers and researchers in universities

scot-homes.gov.uk The Homepage of Scottish Homes, that funds and regulates housing associations in Scotland

sustainablehomes.co.uk Sustainable Homes promotes awareness of sustainable development issues and good practice, and encourages housing associations to adopt sustainable policies and practices. Sustainable Homes is based at Hastoe Housing Association and funded by an Innovation and Good Practice Grant from the Housing Corporation

triodos.co.uk The UK website of Triodos Bank, one of Europe's leading ethical banks who finance initiatives delivering wider social, environmental and cultural benefits.

Note on CoHousing terminology

It may be wondered why the term 'CoHousing' is consistently written with both 'C'and 'H' as capitals, as it was not used in this manner by McCammant & Durrett when they coined the word 'cohousing' in translating the original Danish term 'bofælleskab'. 'Bo' in Danish means both to live, reside and house, and the compound word 'bofælleskab' conveys a subtle combination of 'housed together', 'residing together', and 'living in common'. It is something that is not straightforward to put into an English translation. McCammant & Durrett's word certainly does not appear to have had much use before use of it to refer to the original Danish communities.

In the UK, however, a word that at face value appears to have something to do with 'housing' runs a real risk of being interpreted as just being 'something to do with housing', rather than with what might be the creation of a particular style of mutually-supportive neighbourhood community. The notion of people creating accommodation or neighbourhoods for themselves, especially in common with others, is far removed from the usual business of 'housing' in the UK.

Commentators in the UK who are not clear about what the term 'CoHousing' represents, nevertheless attempt to describe it in terms of those things with which they have some degree of familiarity. This both detracts from a proper understanding of what is necessarily characteristic about CoHousing communities, and leads to the suggestion that such community initiatives have already been attempted, where no such reality exists. One could argue further, that it may suit the 'status quo' to describe 'CoHousing' in conventional terms as no more than similar to what is already in existence, as this may minimise aspirations that something as basic as 'housing' could be radically different from how the industry has traditionally presented its basic values.

The basic reason for writing 'CoHousing' with two capitals is therefore an attempt to make the written word a device that can catch people's attention long enough for them to stop and wonder whether or not they are clear and accurate about what it represents. CoHousing is at times damned by a false comparison with other community initiatives not least because there is insufficient clarity for what is being described. The printed word 'CoHousing' is put forward with its double capitals with the clear intention that it should offer a challenge to what people may think they are already doing with it!

APPENDIX A

Select Bibliography and Contacts

Texts relevant to CoHousing development in the UK:

BRENTON M. (1998) 'We're in charge. 'CoHousing Communities of older people in the Netherlands: lessons for Britain,?. Bristol, Policy Press.

DIGGERS AND DREAMERS : The Guide to Communal Living, D & D Pub

FIELD M (2000) "Targets for Intentional Communities?" 'Axis', Aug/Sep. 2000 issue, and on DETR-sponsored website 'RegenNet'

HANSON C. (1996) The CoHousing Handbook, Hartley & Marks, Point Roberts, USA

THE HOCKERTON COMMUNITY (2001) The Sustainable Community - A Practical Guide. (Website : www.hockerton.demon.co.uk)

HOUSING FOR WOMEN / HOUSING CORPORATION (2002) "The Legal and Financial feasibility of setting up a CoHousing community for older women in London", Housing For Women, London

McCAMANT K & DURRETT C. (1988.rev1994) CoHousing. a contemporary approach to housing ourselves. Berkeley, California. Ten Speed Press.

NEAL P. ed. (2003) Urban Villages and the Making of Communities, Spon Press, London, UK

NELSON L. (1997) CoHousing : Designs for Living, Eco Design, Vol.V, No.2

ROGERS D. & FIELD M. (1998) 'Legal and financial frameworks for CoHousing projects', (in Brenton M. op cit.)

WATES N (2000) The Community Planning Handbook.. Earthscan,

Other texts:

BARTON H. et al (2000) Sustainable Communities, Earthscan, UK

BARTON H. & TSOUROU C (2000) Healthy Urban Planning, Spon Press (on behalf of World Health Organisation)

BIRCHALL J. (1988) Building Communities, the Co-operative Way, Routledge Kegan Paul, UK

BRENTON M. (1999) Choice, autonomy and mutual support: older women's collaborative living arrangements. York: York Publishing Services/Joseph Rowntree Foundation.
(2001) 'Older People's CoHousing Communities' in S.Peace & C.Holland (eds) Inclusive Housing for an Ageing Society'. Bristol, Policy Press.

BROWN T. et al (2000) Stakeholder Housing, Pluto Press, London

CDS Co-operatives, 'Model rules for housing co-operatives'. CDS, 3 Marshalsea Road, London SE1 1EP

CHANON G "Community Responses to Social Exclusion", in Policy Responses to Social Exclusion, Percy-Smith J. et al (2000), OUP

COATES C. (2001) Utopia Britannica, D & D Publications, London

DEPARTMENT OF THE ENVIRONMEN T, TRANSPORT & THE REGIONS
Planning for Communities of the Future, London, HMSO, (1997)
Sustainability Counts (1998)
A Better Quality of Life : the Government's National Sustainable
Development Strategy, (1999)
By Design : Urban Design in the Planning System, (2000)
Local Quality of Life Counts (2000)
Millennium Villages and Sustainable Communities, (2000)
Our Towns and Cities : the future (Urban White Paper), (2000)
Prepare an Effective Local Agenda 21 Strategy , (2000)
Quality and Choice : a decent home for all (Green Paper), (2000)
Sustainable Development Research : Gaps and Opportunities, (2000)
Sustainable Local Communities for the 21st Century : Why and How to
Quality & choice for older people's housing: a strategic framework(2001)

DUFFY K. & HUTCHINSON J.(1997) "Urban policy and the turn to community" Town Planning Review, 68, 347-362

ENO S & TREANOR D (1982) The Collective Housing Handbook,
Laurieston Hall Publications, Castle Douglas, Scotland

FAIRLIE S. (1996) Low Impact Development : Planning and People in a
Sustainable Countryside, Jon Carpenter Publishing, Oxfords.

FIELD M (2001) "Policies to support the creation of new neighbourhood
communities", Proceedings of the 'International Sustainable Development
Research Conference - Manchester, 2001', ERP Environment, Shipley, UK
(2001) "Obstacles to Creating New 'Neighbourhood Communities' in
UK", Paper given to the "International Community Studies Association" in
ZEGG, Berlin, June 2001

FICH M.et al(1995) Old People's Houses, Kunstakademiets Forlag, Cophag

FROMM D. (1991) Collaborative communities : CoHousing, central living
and other forms of housing with shared facilities, Reinhold, New York

GEHL J. (1987) Life Between Buildings, Van Nostrand Reinhold, New York

GINSON T. (1996) The Power in Our Hands, Jon Carpenter, Charlbury, UK

GRAYSON L. (2000) The Housing Challenge : a review of the issues, The
Planning Exchange, Glasgow

HALL P. (1996) Cities of Tomorrow, Blackwell, Oxford, UK

HALL P. & WARD C. (1998) Sociable Cities - the Legacy of Ebenezer
Howard, Wiley, Chichester

HALPERN.D(2004) Social Capital, Polity Press.

HANDY C (1988) Understanding Voluntary Organisations - how to make
them function effectively, Penguin ISBN 0-14-014338-6

HARDY D.(1979) Alternative Communities in Nineteenth Century
England, Longman, New York
(2001)Utopian England: Community Experiments 1900-1945, Spon.London

HEALEY P. (1997) Collaborative Planning, Macmillan, Basingstoke, UK

HILDUR J .(Ed. 1999) Creating Harmony.: conflict resolution in community. Gaia Trust/Permanent pub. ISBN 1-85623-014-7

HOURIET R. (1973) Getting Back Together, Sphere Books, London, UK

HULL A. (1997) "Restructuring the debate on allocating land for housing
growth", Housing Studies, Vol 12, No 3, p367-382

INSTITUTE FOR PUBLIC POLICY RESEARCH (2000), Housing United
:Final Report of the Forum on the Future of Social Housing, IPPR London

LOCAL GOVERNMENT ASSOCIATION (2000), Vision into Reality : the future strategic housing role of local authorities, LGA, London

MARKHAM THORSONS U (1996) Managing Conflict : how to deal with difficult situations at work. Ursula. ISBN 0-7225-3109-5

METCALF B. (1998) "Sustainable communal living around the globe : Yesterday, Today and Tomorrow", paper presented at Creating Sustainable Community Conference, Findhorn, Oct/98

National Housing Federation, Model management agreements for the tenant management of housing owned by an RSL are available from the NHF, 175 Grays Inn Road, London WCIX 5UP.

NORWOOD K. & SMITH K. (1995) Rebuilding Community in America, Shared Living Resource Centre, University of California

ODPM (Office of the Deputy Prime Minister) (2002) Living Places : Cleaner, Safer, Greener, HMSO
(2003) Sustainable communities: building for the future, HMSO,

OSPINA J (1987) Housing Ourselves, Hilary Shipman, London

PEARSON L. (1988) The Architectural & Social History of Co-operative Living, Macmillan, Basingstoke, UK

PERCY-SMITHH J(2000)Policy Responses to Social Exclusion,OUPress UK

THE PRINCE'S FOUNDATION (2000) Sustainable Urban Extensions : Planned through Design, Prince's Foundation/English Partnerships, London

RIGBY A. (1974) Communes in Britain, Routledge Kegan Paul, London

ROOM (2000) Defining Positive Planning : briefing paper for consultation, National Council for Housing and Planning, London

ROSLIN M. & FIELD M. (1998) 'Mini-neighbourhoods', Resurgence, No.190

SCHWARZ W. & D. (1998) Living Lightly : Travels in Post-consumer Society, Jon Carpenter, Charlbury, UK

SOCIAL EXCLUSION UNIT (2001) A New Commitment to Neighbourhood Renewal : National Strategy Action Plan, London, HMSO

SOMERVILLE P. (1998) "Empowerment through residence", Housing Studies, Vol 13, No 2, p233-257

STOCKDALE A. & LLOYD G. (1998) "Forgotten Needs? The demographic and socio-economic impact of free-standing new settlements", Housing Studies, Vol 13, No 1, p43-58

STUTLEY R. (2001) The Definitive Business Plan, Prentice Hall, US

TURNER J (1976) Housing by People - Towards Autonomy in Building Environments, Marion Boyars, London

URBAN DESIGN GROUP Urban Design Source Book, UDG, London

URBAN TASK FORCE (1999) Towards an Urban Renaissance, London,

WARD C. (1990) Talking Houses, Freedom Press, London
(1996) Talking to Architects, Freedom Press, London

YOUNG M. & LEMOS G. (1997) The Communities We Have Lost and Can Regain, Lemos & Crane, London

ZAHLE K. & MORTENSEN P.D. (1992) "Collective and Co-operative Housing", Open House International, Vol.17, No.2, p56-65

Key Websites:

buildingforlife.org Building for Life is a commitment to the quality of new homes made by 3 key partners: the house-building industry, represented by the House Builders Federation ; government, represented by the Commission for Architecture & the Built Environment (CABE); and campaigners, represented by the Civic Trust

cch.coop Website of the Confederation of Co-operative Housing - the UK organisation for housing co-operatives, tenant-controlled housing organisations and regional federations of housing co-ops.

charity-commission.gov.uk Registrar of Charities website, main source of information on legal documents, charity structures.

cohousing.co.uk A window on the cohousing scene in the UK covering existing and forming groups. Carries ads for groups looking for new members and properties for sale in exisiting Cohousing schemes as well as various discussion papers.

cohousing.org The Cohousing Association of the United States (Coho/US) is an organization whose purpose is to promote and encourage the cohousing concept, support both individuals and groups in creating communities, provide assistance to completed groups for improving their systems for living together in community, and provide networking opportunities for those involved or interested in cohousing.

communitiestakingcontrol.org This site is about communities in England setting up community initiatives to tackle issues important to local communities. The site is primarily aimed at tenants of housing associations, but because it is about a wide range of community control opportunities, much of the information will be relevant to tenants and communities in general.

companieshouse.gov.uk Main registration authority for companies and source of public information.

ctegrants.org.uk Community Training & Enabling grants are designed to support housing association residents in England to develop new training and community development projects.

diggersanddreamers.org.uk If you're interested in joining or setting up some kind of intentional community then this is thewebsitefor you. you'll find news, views and other useful resources including a fully searchable database of communities in Britain.

fsa.gov.uk The Financial Services Agency aims to maintain efficient, orderly and clean financial markets and help retail consumers achieve a fair deal. It aims to help consumers become better informed about financial matters, for example with information on : endowment mortgages; advice on comparative mortgages; consumer help; resources for Teaching and Learning

hbf.co.uk The House Builders Federation (HBF) is the principal trade federation for private sector housebuilders and voice of the house building industry in England and Wales.

housingcorp.gov.uk The Homepage of the Housing Corporation, that funds and regulates housing associations in England and Wales **jrf.org.uk** The Joseph Rowntree Foundation is one of the largest social policy research and development charities in the UK. It spends about £7 million a year on a research and development programme that seeks to better understand the causes of social difficulties and explore ways of better overcoming them. It also engages in practical housing and care work through the Joseph Rowntree Housing Trust, and is currently involved in the planning of a new 540-home housing development in York.

lease-advice.org The Leasehold Advisory Service is an independent advice agency, funded by Government grant. It provides free advice to leaseholders, landlords, professional advisers and others on the law affecting residential leasehold property.

nihe.gov.uk Homepage of the Northern Ireland Housing executive, that funds and regulates housing associations in Northern Ireland.

princes-foundation.org The Prince's Foundation for the Built Environment is an educational charity established by The Prince of Wales to teach and demonstrate in practice those principles of traditional urban design and architecture which put people and the communities of which they are part at the centre of the design process. The website includes the detail of the new 'Urban Network' which has replaced the Urban Villages Forum.

regen.net Information network for mutli-agency partnerships involved in urban regeneration, rural regeneration, economic development and community development.

rtpi.org.uk The RTPI exists to advance the science and art of town planning for the benefit of the public.
It is a membership organisation, and a registered charity. Most of its members are fully qualified professional planners. Nearly two thirds work as planning officers for local councils. Others work for central government, for property developers and other organisations with significant landholdings, as consultants or as teachers and researchers in universities

scot-homes.gov.uk The Homepage of Scottish Homes, that funds and regulates housing associations in Scotland

sustainablehomes.co.uk Sustainable Homes promotes awareness of sustainable development issues and good practice, and encourages housing associations to adopt sustainable policies and practices. Sustainable Homes is based at Hastoe Housing Association and funded by an Innovation and Good Practice Grant from the Housing Corporation

triodos.co.uk The UK website of Triodos Bank, one of Europe's leading ethical banks who finance initiatives delivering wider social, environmental and cultural benefits.

Note on CoHousing terminology

It may be wondered why the term 'CoHousing' is consistently written with both 'C'and 'H' as capitals, as it was not used in this manner by McCammant & Durrett when they coined the word 'cohousing' in translating the original Danish term 'bofælleskab'. 'Bo' in Danish means both to live, reside and house, and the compound word 'bofælleskab' conveys a subtle combination of 'housed together', 'residing together', and 'living in common'. It is something that is not straightforward to put into an English translation. McCammant & Durrett's word certainly does not appear to have had much use before use of it to refer to the original Danish communities.

In the UK, however, a word that at face value appears to have something to do with 'housing' runs a real risk of being interpreted as just being 'something to do with housing', rather than with what might be the creation of a particular style of mutually-supportive neighbourhood community. The notion of people creating accommodation or neighbourhoods for themselves, especially in common with others, is far removed from the usual business of 'housing' in the UK.

Commentators in the UK who are not clear about what the term 'CoHousing' represents, nevertheless attempt to describe it in terms of those things with which they have some degree of familiarity. This both detracts from a proper understanding of what is necessarily characteristic about CoHousing communities, and leads to the suggestion that such community initiatives have already been attempted, where no such reality exists. One could argue further, that it may suit the 'status quo' to describe 'CoHousing' in conventional terms as no more than similar to what is already in existence, as this may minimise aspirations that something as basic as 'housing' could be radically different from how the industry has traditionally presented its basic values.

The basic reason for writing 'CoHousing' with two capitals is therefore an attempt to make the written word a device that can catch people's attention long enough for them to stop and wonder whether or not they are clear and accurate about what it represents. CoHousing is at times damned by a false comparision with other community initiatives not least because there is insufficient clarity for what is being described. The printed word 'CoHousing' is put forward with its double capitals with the clear intention that it should offer a challenge to what people may think they are already doing with it!

Printed in the United Kingdom
by Lightning Source UK Ltd.
101658UKS00001B/70-156